A Financial Advancement Designed with the Investor in Mind

Robert L. Evans

Disclaimer

TABLE OF CONTENTS

NAMES AND ACRONYMS
"THE EQUITY RESCUE PROGRAM" ©

Equity Rescue is the name of the program that features the rescue of property equities from foreclosure. Within the Equity Rescue Program is:

THE "EQUITY GROWTH LIMITED PARTNERSHIP© (EGLP)" ©

That has two classes of limited partners, one class called the Privilege Cash Investor Limited Partner (PCI), another called the Equity Growth Partner Limited Partner (EGP)

"THE TRUST DEED PLEDGE PLAN© (TDPP)" ©

is a real estate transaction that operates within the EGLP with a legal, financial, and investment original design structure. The TDPP features a way to cure a foreclosure and rescue the owner's equity and it creates a new investor and investment technique.

LIMITED PARTNERS IN THE EGLP/TDPP

In the Equity Growth Limited Partnership (EGLP) there is an Equity Growth Partner (EGP) limited partner, an owner of property in a foreclosure process. The EGLP features the distinctive Deed of Trust Pledge Plan (TDPP) with a far advanced investment innovation included. A secured Privilege Cash Investor (PCI) position is featured that has an investment status and legal position second to none. There are individual sections for the FORECLOSURE OWNER, EGLP, TDPP, PCI, LEGAL, and special personal EARNING summary.

THE FOLLOWING ABBREVIATIONS ARE USED:

- EGLP is an Equity Growth Limited Partnership
- PCI is a Privileged Cash Investor, a Limited Partner in an EGLP
- EGP is an Equity Growth Partner, a Limited Partner in an EGLP
- TDPP is the Trust Deed Pledge Plan, a plan operating within an EGLP
- PTD is the Performance Trust Deed

INTRODUCTION

This writing explains what the Equity Rescue transaction does, how it works and is structured. The word "foreclosure" is used in the Equity Rescue Program and if you're like most people, negative thoughts about this subject are filling your mind right about now. Stop. Wait a moment. Don't apply such thoughts to Equity Rescue because Equity Rescue is an innovative and much better method of dealing with real estate foreclosures. The old understandings of how people deal with foreclosure simply do not apply to Equity Rescue. The transaction is called the Trust Deed Pledge Plan (TDPP).

Would you agree that there is a continual need for investment capital? Would you agree that people need a real solution to foreclosure, that is, one that allows them to avoid the loss of their money? If you answered, "yes" to both questions then you are going to appreciate the Equity Rescue Program. Equity Rescue addresses these two "needs" like no other answer before it ever has.

Many years in real estate practice in several areas of real estate highlighted the suffering that occurs regularly from foreclosure. In many cases, a large amount of money is lost by the property owner when a foreclosure occurs. Money that was earned supporting the property over many years. It is devastating for the owner and ugly to watch. Real Estate Brokers often see property owners lose their financial nest egg earned for retirement because they have no equitable answer. This constant, never-ending loss of property equity became paramount to developing an acceptable answer.

Many answers to solve a foreclosure are claimed. Some are "negotiate with the lender", make a "short sale", or give "a deed in lieu of foreclosure". None of these so-called answers creates any money with which the property owner can solve the foreclosure to save their property equity. Instead, they give up suggestions and do not help the owner. These unreal answers where the owner's only hurtful choices until the Equity Rescue Program was developed.

The "Trust Deed Pledge Plan" (TDPP) in the Equity Growth Limited Partnership (EGLP) is an original real estate "investment transaction" design. The TDPP is designed to produce investment capital to solve various difficult real estate property financial problems, not just a foreclosure problem. The legal, financial, and investment advancements in the EGLP are unique in many respects. They provide avenues and methods of operations never envisioned. Seldom does a discovery yield so much opportunity.

Rescuing property equities and establishing a way to gather very large amounts of investment capital to solve difficult investment problems are both major achievements. The way the TDPP technical innovation in the EGLP is arranged fosters outstanding financial and investment ability. The individual legal, financial, and investment structures introduced in an EGLP are serious carefully throughout advancements. A General Partner of a limited partnership without the same technical tools that have been designed could not offer the same ability.

It is human nature to ask is this transaction something original or something that already exists that I know already. Answer: It is the latest discovery developed in the real estate industry! No one likes to spend time on something already known! What the TDPP in the EGLP does not do, in case you are wondering:

    1) Equity Sharing
    2) Foreclosure speculating for profit
    3) Short Sales
    4) Flipping property in any way
    5) Modification of the loan on the property

GENERAL FORECLOSURE INFORMATION

WHAT FORECLOSURE IS AND MEANS

The technical meaning of the word is to wipe out a right of redemption on a property. Generally, this happens when someone does not pay their mortgage. Even though there have been no payments, the borrower retains an equitable right of redemption if someday they can find the money and try to exercise their right of redemption. To clear the title of this potential, a lender goes to court, demonstrates the default, and requests that a date be set where the entire amount becomes payable, after which, in the absence of payment, the lender is automatically relieved of the requirement to redeem the property back to the borrower; the debtor's right of redemption is said to be forever barred and foreclosed. This cancels all rights a borrower would have in the property, and the property then belongs entirely to the lender, who is then free to possess or sell the property. The word is frequently used to refer to the lender's actions of repossessing and selling a property for default in mortgage payments.

A BETTER WAY TO SOLVE FORECLOSURE

The word "foreclosure" for many people automatically has a negative connotation. However, in the case of the Equity Rescue Program, any negative assumption one might make because of its involvement with foreclosure does not apply. The foundation of this fresh approach is a very positive attitude towards helping the property owner in foreclosure. Equity Rescue rescues all the property equity from foreclosure for the owner, and the entire equity rescued grows with profit share. Also, all the negative financial and legal consequences a foreclosure causes are eliminated for the owners. And there is no charge to the owner for the service and use of the intellectual plan provided to rescue the equity.

FORECLOSURE REALLY HURTS

As each person's financial well-being is paramount, establishing an earning system that will build wealth is critical. An established way in the United States of America to earn and build a comfortable retirement fund is to own real estate that will increase in value over time. Millions of Americans use this method to be financially secure later in life. However, a foreclosure can cause a complete loss of property equity if the loan is not paid on time as agreed.

Each year hundreds of thousands of property owners throughout the United States lose their nest eggs planned for retirement through foreclosure. Here is the very standard everyday foreclosure problem; a property owner goes into foreclosure with a substantial amount of equity in the property and no way to financially solve the foreclosure. The owner will then be subject to giving away a sale for pennies on the dollar or to losing the equity in a forced foreclosure auction. These are the only two choices an owner has if the owner does not have or cannot borrow the money to cure the default. Equity Rescue can now help the owner save all the equity from foreclosure.

Foreclosure is a serious problem for the owner that society has been concerned with since the beginning. No fair and acceptable answer to foreclosure for the owner has ever been found until now. Now there is a fair and honest way to solve a foreclosure and rescue the equity for the property owners. The Equity Rescue Program Trust Deed Pledge Plan (TDPP) provides a groundbreaking avenue for owners to receive financial help of foreclosure. As property equities are rescued from foreclosure, real estate brokers, lenders, and bankruptcy courts will benefit financially. First-time job opportunities that provide financial benefit for many adds to the special value of the plan.

A fact that is unchallengeable. In the United States, there are billions and billions of dollars lost by property owners because of foreclosure. History teaches and confirms this. Foolish to argue with a fact that is indisputable.

Poor distribution of earnings causes foreclosure! When it is realized that 43% of American households spend more than they earn each year and 60% or more live from paycheck to paycheck, it is not difficult to understand why so many property owners go into foreclosure each year!

Here are some of the reasons that cause an owner to go into foreclosure, Divorce, Drugs, Death, College Costs, Poor Money Management, Medical Bills, Bad Business Decisions, Market Trends, All Kinds of Accidents, Lower Income Due to Lay Offs or Job Loss, Adjustable Monthly Payment Increases, Lending Trends, Bad Practices, Etc.

The century-old foreclosure process of closing out property ownership and causing the owner to lose the property equity will continue forever. There is no other way to protect the money loaned on the property by the lender when an owner cannot pay as agreed. There are hundreds of thousands of Default Notices that start the foreclosure process sent to property owners each year in the United States. There has never been a positive solution for property owners in the United States in this circumstance until the Equity Rescue Program.

The remedies offered in the marketplace for property in the foreclosure process are of no financial help to the owners. The owner can arrange a give-away-sale price and suffer the property's equity loss. Or the owner's property is sold at a forced foreclosure auction that will cause the loss of the equity. The TDPP is the only positive financial answer for the owner who cannot cure the pending foreclosure themselves.

PART 1
PROPERTY OWNER IN FORECLOSURE

FROM PENDING DISASTER TO A NEW START

The Equity Growth Partner (EGP) is a new type of limited partner "property investor" in the EGLP/TDPP. Sometimes referred herein to just the property "owner". Even though the owner is in foreclosure financial trouble, it becomes possible for the owner to save all the property equity to invest. The foreclosed owner becomes a qualified cash investor in an EGLP after the property equity is rescued from foreclosure. This owner conversion to a qualified investor is the foundation of a new way to raise EGLP operating and investment capital on a never-ending always-increasing basis. While helping people solve their foreclosure problems can be a very rewarding and gratifying experience, the main purpose of Equity Rescue is to raise operating and investment capital. The EGLP can earn profit for itself and all the property owners, that were once in foreclosure and have become EGLP limited partners investors.

A DIFFERENT INVESTMENT FOR THE PROPERTY OWNER

Equity Rescue's plan is groundbreaking in that it features a way to solve the serious foreclosure problem. The plan is for the owner who does not have or cannot find the money to solve the foreclosure Notice of Default (NOD). With a new, never-before constructed legal method specially designed to achieve helping a property owner, it becomes possible for the property owner with a serious money problem to solve the problem. By joining Equity Rescue to rescue the equity, the owner becomes a qualified investor in an EGLP. The EGLP rescues the equity for the owner without charge and allows the owner to grow the equity substantially to ensure future purchasing power.

THE SCARY FORECLOSURE NOTICE OF DEFAULT

A pending foreclosure against property, if completed, cause the owner very serious legal and financial consequences such as:

- A loss of the entire equity remaining in the property,
- A harsh long-term financing cost and credit damage because of a foreclosure,
- A loss of investor status and future earnings,
- A position of no money, no credit, and no place to live,
- A problem of earning the same amount of equity lost over again,
- A potential lawsuit from a junior lender holding the note after the foreclosure wiped out the lender's lien on the property,
- A capital gain tax after foreclosure without the money (property equity) to pay the tax,
- The owner needs to avoid all these nasty foreclosure consequences by joining the EGLP/TDPP.

FORECLOSURE: WHO IS TO BLAME

What causes a foreclosure? The financial activity of the general economy affects the number of foreclosures. However, some reasons causing foreclosure to have nothing to do with the real estate market trends and will always make foreclosures go on and on. Financial problems causing foreclosure are Divorce, Drugs, Death, Poor Money Management, Medical Bills, College Costs, Accidents, Bad Business Decisions, Bad Business Market Trends, Employment Displacement Causing Lower Income, High-rate Interest Only Loans, and Loan Payments that are in flux because of Adjustable Rate. These problems will never go away and will be repeated daily by the thousands throughout the United States forever.

NO OTHER ANSWER SAVES THE OWNER'S EQUITY

No other fair real answer is offered or possible! Many answers to solve a foreclosure are claimed by individuals. Some are "negotiate with the lender", make a "short sale", or give "a deed in lieu of foreclosure". Of course, none of these so called "answers" create any money with which the owners can even begin to "solve" the foreclosure and save their credit and property equity. Instead, they are "stalling" or "give up techniques" and, in the final analysis, do not help the property owners in foreclosure.

There is a "Foreclosure Profit Speculator System" throughout the United States that takes financial advantage of an owner in foreclosure in no uncertain terms. The profit speculator takes advantage of the owner by telling the owner that the owner's credit will be saved by avoiding foreclosure. The buyer does nothing else for the owner/seller. The buyer takes the property ownership for a few dollars, pays pennies on the dollar and takes several thousands of dollars of the owner's property equity. It is like being a bank robber without going to prison. Profit speculating about foreclosure is not a nice thing for the owner. However, it is not against the law and the speculator did not cause the owner problem!

A REAL AND HONEST ANSWER

The EGLP/TDPP is a welcome answer for the millions and millions of property owners who will face foreclosure in the coming years. It will help property owners, lenders, and real estate professionals gain substantial benefits because it introduces a new and better way to solve a pending foreclosure and invest safely. This new avenue is sorely needed and has been created to help people and businesses in need of a fair and just answer to the foreclosure problem.

For owners who are in the foreclosure process, the EGLP/TDPP turns a pending misfortune into a real solution by providing a positive answer. By arranging a set of unique legal, financial, and investment advantages for the owners in the plan, designed especially for their situation, the EGLP/TDPP can help the owners avoid the foreclosure and loss of their property equity. The TDPP helps the owner from incurring harsh costs over the long-term because of the credit problem a concluded foreclosure would cause. Also, any loan balance, tax, or legal problem a foreclosure would cause is completely and totally avoided by the owner.

Honesty and doing it the right way. Scamming the owner in foreclosure makes the word foreclosure a nasty word. The state and federal foreclosure laws that control "negative foreclosure actions", by unscrupulous cheats, do not apply to the activity that equity rescue is involved in! The TDPP in the EGLP solves the foreclosure, rescues all the equity entirely for the owner's benefit, and pays the investor's bonus for the owner out of EGLP's gross investment profit earned. No owner money is ever taken from the owner by the PCI or EGLP, the TDPP is free of any cost for the owner! Equity Rescue works to educate and improve what happens to an uneducated first-time troubled owner in the foreclosure process. In the EGLP the owner, the investor and the EGLP are all recipients of financial benefits of the TDPP. That is what is important, everyone wins!

PEOPLE'S LACK OF KNOWLEDGE

Many people not familiar with the foreclosure process think that because the property has some equity, it is still possible to sell it and save the equity. The market does not work this way! What really happens in the market? Once a property has a Notice of Default filed against it, the offer to buy amount equals the loan amount plus a few thousand dollars that a buyer or speculator will offer. The low offer is because of the distressed foreclosure situation the owner is in. Upon the NOD being filed in the land record office, the property market value immediately drops drastically. It's a fact!

Human nature dictates the same result time and time again! When a person purchases a product, service or real estate property, they look to get the best price possible. That happens because the buyer always looks to buy for the lowest price so profit can be maximized. No one walks up to an owner and says, "Because you are in dire financial straits, I will pay the full market value for your property."

A potential buyer does not pay a fair price for a property under duress of a foreclosure. The buyer will take the owner's equity earned by faithfully making loan payments for little or nothing every time. Centuries of behavior teach this very clearly, and it will never change! The property equity took the owners years to accumulate by faithfully making loan payments on time. It is a terrible blow to lose the equity after paying so much to create the equity position. The owner in many cases suffers the loss of their retirement financial nest egg.

SERIOUS FORECLOSURE SITUATION FOR THE OWNER

When a property has a foreclosure pending the owner becomes vulnerable to the pressure of time, lack of money, and the owner's financial standing. This combination together makes the default extremely difficult to solve. The owner is in an untenable situation that requires money and timely attention that the owner does not have. The financial duress the owner is under makes it impossible to sell the real estate for full market value. The plan is for the owner who does not have or cannot find the money to solve the foreclosure Notice of Default (NOD) on time.

No other "financial relief" except for the EGLP/TDPP is available for hundreds of thousands of foreclosures that occur each year throughout the United States each year. Foreclosure happens daily in the United States and has been going on for centuries. There is a long history of billions of dollars lost by the owners each year. Every owner with property equity to close due to financial constraints caused by foreclosure needs the Equity Rescue Program answer. By joining the EGLP, the owner's total property equity is rescued without charge of any kind. Only Equity Rescue exclusively has and can provide the answer to the problem for property owners.

By joining a unique legal, financial, and investment arrangement, the owner avoids the foreclosure and loss of equity and all the negative consequences a foreclosure might cause. Any loan balance, tax, or legal problem a foreclosure would cause is completely extinguished for the owner. The owner immediately eliminates the horror of foreclosure and gains the opportunity to improve their current and future financial status. Equity Rescue offers the owners the most attractive foreclosure equity loss solution available anywhere!

THE FORECLOSURE OWNER'S SITUATION

The owners in foreclosure are faced with many serious problems and must join Equity Rescue or suffer serious consequences. The owner needs to solve all these serious problems, and only the EGLP/TDPP can do it.
The owner has:
- A mortgage payment is several months behind.
- No personal funds with which to cure the foreclosure.
- No borrowing is possible on the highly leveraged property.
- Personal credit disqualifies the owner due to the default notice on the property.
- Little time to find money to pay the loan arrearage and related costs.
- A long-term expensive financing problem due to a negative credit report.
- A capital gains tax if any is due after the foreclosure occurs.
- A lack of ability to negotiate an "arms-length" fair price property sale.

- A lack of any solution in the marketplace that benefits the owner.
- An extreme position with no solution and no knowledge of how to rescue the equity.
- A possible note collection lawsuit against the owner from a junior loan lender whose security was wiped out.

THE OWNER NEEDS A LOT
The owner needs:
- To find an infusion of cash immediately to cure a pending foreclosure at a time when the owner is financially insolvent and has no borrowing power.
- To find a plan and professional help to immediately lower the risk by curing the foreclosure.
- To find a plan to rescue the equity cost-free.
- To immediately lower the owner's risk by curing the foreclosure.
- To rescue the property equity and gain time to restructure personal credit and financial standing.
- To invest and make the money grow during the personal financial restructuring period.
- To eliminate the monthly payment and the loan principal.
- To retain equity and grow the equity for future purchasing power.

The TDPP helps people in dire financial straits immediately eliminate the horror of foreclosure and gain control of their financial status. After becoming financially sound by avoiding foreclosure, owners can begin taking steps towards total financial recovery. The Equity Rescue Program offers the owners an attractive foreclosure equity loss solution for the first-time ever!

THE DIFFICULT MONEY PROBLEM
The financial status of a typical property owner in foreclosure. The owner needs to find the money to solve the foreclosure in a very limited time. The property's debt structure is highly leveraged, and the owner is financially insolvent due to a pending foreclosure. Under these circumstances, borrowing more money to cure a foreclosure is very difficult. This leaves the owner searching for a friend or relative to lend the money to save a substantial amount of equity in the property. The owner's effort generally fails as their borrowing ability is next to nil while in foreclosure. This situation occurs "hundreds of thousands of times yearly" in the United States. History tells us the high number of foreclosures that occur each year will continue to happen!

Money is the problem! The owner is bewildered without an actual foreclosure experience that forms a correct understanding of what is happening. It is difficult for a person to understand the legal and financial foreclosure process that is happening to them. Owners unfamiliar with the foreclosure process think that because the property has twenty or thirty percent equity, it is still possible to borrow against it to cure the foreclosure. Lending more money may bring the total owing to eighty percent LTV or higher with a total larger monthly payment. The private lenders and financial institutions have rules and regulations and need security in the form of enough equity to protect themselves. It is difficult for a lender to justify loaning more money when the borrower has not paid current monthly payments. It is extremely difficult for the owner to borrow more money and pay it back on time.

If a property has a 75% or higher LTV (loan to value), private equity lenders, called hard money lenders, will not loan more funds against the property. This is because there needs to be a cushion represented in the remaining amount of equity to protect the new loan amount. And the owner must qualify income wise to borrow more money. This general rule goes for all lenders making any kind of loan. The lender must be concerned about the owner going into bankruptcy. A bankruptcy would wipe out much of the equity due to the fact the owner does not pay the loan payments during the stalling period a bankruptcy would cause. Then there are court costs and attorney fees. And the lender does not want to be accused of lending too much to encourage a future foreclosure, so that it looks like the lender did it on purpose to gain financially from a lender foreclosure.

Regular lending institutions such as savings and loans will not lend into a Notice of Default recorded against a property. Banks have state and federal rules and regulations to abide by and stockholders that frown on lending more money to a property that has a defaulted loan against it. This adds to the serious problem for the owner, who needs to borrow funds against a property to solve a pending foreclosure.

This leaves the owner in foreclosure, searching for a friend, relative, or company to lend the money needed to cure the foreclosure. If these sources are not forthcoming, the owner will suffer a give-away sale for pennies on a dollar or will go to a forced sale by the lender at auction. Either way, the owner's equity in the property is lost. This foreclosure situation repeatedly occurs for owners without a personal money answer. The owner has substantial equity with no way to save it! The owner needs Equity Rescue to find the money needed to save their property equity (money), wouldn't you think?

MONEY ANSWER FOR THE PROPERTY OWNER

The desperate need for many thousands of property owners in America to avoid foreclosure and rescue all their property equity is answered. The TDPP has been designed to provide the money to rescue the property equity from foreclosure for the owner who does not have the money to solve a pending foreclosure. The EGLP/TDPP provides money to cure the foreclosure, rescue the equity, and make the owner into a qualified investor to grow the rescued equity. The special ability to rescue the equity and make it grow has never been designed before now.

Equity Rescue will help many owners who have defaulted on their loan(s) by solving their foreclosure money problem. The solution will improve, a great deal, their immediate and future financial position. There has never been an acceptable way to solve a foreclosure for the owners other than the owners curing the foreclosure themselves, which benefits the owners.

One who reads about the Equity Rescue Program should realize there is no other way to rescue all the property equity from foreclosure for the owner! The unique legal, financial, and investment physical structures within the EGLP have never been developed before and are the reason the property equity rescue can take place.

EGLP/TDPP SOLVES THE OWNER'S PROBLEM

Exceptional original benefits are arranged in the EGLP/TDPP for the owner.
The owner can now gain by:

- Having the pending foreclosure cured immediately.
- Accomplishing an arms-length full-value sale.
- Making the owner into a qualified investor sharing EGLP net profit.
- Having all (100%) their property equity rescued.
- Growing the rescued equity to increase the owner's future purchasing power.
- Having the total loan balance paid off.
- Gaining time to reorganize to re-establish credit and personal income.
- Avoiding all the negative financial consequences a foreclosure causes, such as long-term bad credit, potential lawsuits, and a need to save the money that would be lost.
- Offering free use of the Equity Rescue Program's exclusive plan and expertise of the general partner.

AVOIDING IS AS IMPORTANT AS SOLVING

Here are ugly financial and legal consequences the owner benefits from by:

- Avoiding incurring harsh long-term financing costs, a concluded foreclosure would cause.
- Avoiding the loss the entire equity in the property.
- Avoiding ten years of expensive credit damage.
- Avoiding a potential lawsuit from a junior lender wiped out by the foreclosure.
- Avoiding loss of investment leverage.
- Avoiding loss of an earning opportunity by arranging to invest in a different way.
- Avoiding starting over with no money and no credit.

NOTE: When you consider that these things are avoided for the owner, at no cost to the owner, it becomes clear that the EGLP/TDPP is indeed providing a very big helping hand at a critical moment in-time for the owner. Do you think the owner would choose to lose the money or save and grow the rescued equity using the TDPP in the EGLP?

HOW THE EGLP/TDPP DOES IT

New methods and techniques:

- The funds are introduced in the plan in a way that never existed before to cure a Notice of Default on a property with equity to lose.
- For the first time a pledge of property fee ownership (free of foreclosure) as collateral for the PCI.
- A PCI design that features an original secured investment design in a partnership.
- A new legal structure to accomplish the equity rescue.
- Grants the PCI several legal investment positions that provide extraordinary protection.
- Uses a Performance Trust Deed for the PCI in a different way.
- Sets up a secured transaction for the PCI limited partner.
- The plan arranges a different pay structure for the cash investor.
- The plan arranges a series of legal and financial privileges to protect and reward the PCI.
- The plan arranges for the rescued equity to grow substantially.
- The plan arranges a full value sale of the property taken out of foreclosure.
- The plan arranges for a financially insolvent owner to be a qualified cash investor sharing profit.
- The plan arranges an investor status for the owner.
- The plan arranges an "arms-length" sale by the owner instead of a low-ball sale under duress.
- The plan arranges a much lower investment risk factor compared to other investments.

MANY PROBLEM PROPERTY CATEGORIES CAN BE SOLVED

EGLP/TDPP has answers for financially troubled properties like:

1. Foreclosure Properties
2. Negative Cash Flow Portfolios
3. Earthquake Retrofit Properties
4. Investment Portfolio Properties
5. Tax Problem Properties
6. Brownfield Properties.
7. Any financial problem property.

THE OWNER'S COMMITMENT

The owner agrees to:

- Sell the property through the EGLP.

- Invest the rescued equity in the EGLP. The owner/investor capital (equity) invested is used to operate and invest for profit by the EGLP.
- The owner will pay loan payments until a property is sold by the EGLP, if possible.
- The owner offers the property ownership as collateral to secure the PCI funds invested.
- The owner agrees to lose the property and the equity if it does not sell.
- The owner agrees to give ownership to the PCI, if it becomes necessary.

THE OWNER'S RETURN

The owner's problems are resolved:
- The EGLP/TDPP cures foreclosure.
- A high-risk legal and financial foreclosure position is eliminated.
- The EGLP rescues 100% of the property equity for the owner from foreclosure.
- All the very serious negative consequences of a foreclosure are eliminated.
- The owner gains financial and legal stability immediately to re-establish credit and income.
- The owner is made into a qualified investor in the EGLP upon joining.
- A share of profit grows the owner's rescued equity and gains future purchasing power to invest.
- Monthly payments are eliminated, and the total property loan balance is paid off.
- The owner can stay in the property until it is sold.
- The owner gets money to move and pay new rent to start.
- The owner generates future purchasing power with profit earned.
- The owner avoids a long-term credit problem.
- The owner does not pay a dime for the plan and the professional help provided.

THE OWNER'S COST

The owner's cost to cure the foreclosure and sell the property comes initially from the investor's investment fund in the Partnership. The funds used are reimbursed from the property proceeds when the property sells. As well the standard costs of sale are paid by the owner out of the property equity when the property sells. The owner's actual costs are as follows:
- The owner pays for three professional property reports to attract a qualified investor.
- Pays the money to reinstate the Property's defaulted loan.
- Pays cost to fix up the Property to sell.
- The owner pays the normal sale and closing costs.
- Question? What is the owner's cost of not joining! In the final analysis, the EGLP pays the PCI a $25,500 Bonus, not the owner. Image having someone pay for you to rescue your money!

SAVING THE FINANCIAL FUTURE

Never before Equity Rescue could the owner in a difficult process of foreclosure, that the owner cannot solve, cure the foreclosure and rescue all their equity (money) to invest. The purpose of the property owner joining the TDPP in the EGLP is to save the property equity from foreclosure and invest it to earn future income!

The owner can now have the notice of default cured, accomplish a full value sale, maintain an investor status, have all their equity rescued, grow the rescued equity, generate future purchasing power, have the total loan balance paid off, gain time to reorganize, avoid all the ugly financial and legal consequences that an actual foreclosure occurring creates, while not paying a dime for the help provided.

A BETTER FORECLOSURE ANSWER

The EGLP addresses a cash investment improvement and a property owner's foreclosure problem. The EGLP/TDPP investment configuration affords a property owner in foreclosure and a qualified cash investor (PCI) a unique way to "safely invest together" as limited partners. It offers a positive solution that will rescue "all" of the property equity from a pending foreclosure for the owner. The EGLP offers a fresh financial start for the owners by turning the currently financial insolvent owners into qualified investors. The investment capital gathered is invested for the benefit of the property owners rescued from foreclosure. The EGLP pays a profit share to the owner and grows the owner's rescued equity. Equity Rescue offers the owners the most attractive foreclosure equity loss solution available anywhere!

OWNER MARKET CHOICES

The only choices current market practices afford the owner, who cannot solve the foreclosure himself or herself, are financial disasters for the owners. The owner can sell the property, under duress of a pending foreclosure, at a below market value and take a severe loss which is a terrible choice. Or the owner will lose the property to a foreclosure trustee sale, another disaster for the owner. Going to a "Foreclosure Trustee Sale" is not an acceptable answer for the owners in foreclosure, with this type of finality they lose most or all the equity they have build-up over the years.

The owner by choosing to become a qualified real estate investor in an EGLP can make their capital grow and avoid all the negative consequences of foreclosure. It is not only the present but the future that could be a serious financial problem for the foreclosed owner. For those who find they have run out of solutions and time to avoid a giveaway sale or forced sale, the Equity Rescue program offers the only viable alternative.

Never in the real estate foreclosure market has developed a plan where the owner of the property being foreclosed upon could obtain a full value price for the property. Now the owner has a real choice of selling their property for full value and investing the rescued money by choosing the TDPP. This one-of-a- kind opportunity is the only positive choice for an owner who cannot solve the problem. By joining an EGLP as a limited partner the owner attracts the necessary money and time with which to restructure his present and future financial status.

WOULD YOU JOIN

Question: Would you join the Equity Rescue Program to cure a foreclosure if you were about to lose all your equity and suffer severe financial consequences for many years to come? Or would you rather rescue all your equity, avoid foreclosure and grow your equity in a financially sound limited partnership? Most owners will join to help themselves out of a terrible financial jam. The TDPP gives the owner a choice that would be difficult to say no to! The alternative is a give-away sale or a forced sale at auction which would be devastating in every way for the owner.

JOINING THE EGLP/TDPP

The owner in foreclosure is faced with a serious problem! The owner must join the Equity Rescue TDPP or suffer serious financial consequences that a foreclosure auction or a give-away sale would cause. By joining, the owner becomes a qualified real estate investor in an EGLP and saves and grows their equity capital while simultaneously avoiding all the long-term negative consequences of foreclosure. The owner joining the EGLP can attract the necessary money and time to restructure his current negative financial standing and build a strong financial future. The owner gets a fresh financial start and avoids having to start over again with no credit or money.

The owners are transformed from financially insolvent investors into a suitable investor position. In addition to rescuing the equity of the TDPP, through the owner investing in the TDPP, the amount of the rescued equity increases with a EGLP profit share. The potential consequence, such as having to pay capital gains taxes with no property to sell to pay the taxes with because of a potential of a junior lien lawsuit that has been wiped out, entirely avoided. The opportunity to sell the property at full price and avoid all the nasty consequences of foreclosure are now available using the EGLP/TDPP.

HOW THE OWNER JOINS THE TDPP

- **Step 1** The owner reviews a Preliminary Understand and agrees to the terms offered. (Note: no legal contract is made at this point)
- **Step 2** The GP, for the owner, arranges for 3 professional reports on the property.
- **Step 3** The owner waits until the cash investor (PCI) approves the property using the three professional reports to do so. The GP must also approve the reports.
- **Step 4** Upon approval of the property the owner signs the Articles of Partnership and deposits the property title into the escrow handling the start of the EGLP, simultaneously. (This is the only legal binding contract between the parties.)
- **Step 5** The owner becomes a qualified "cash" investor when the EGLP cures the foreclosure and sells the property at a fair market price. The rescued equity acts as the owner's investment capital in the EGLP. (Now, the owners are financially much safer.)
- **Step 6** The owner waits for the EGLP to invest the funds. Depending on which date the EGP joins, the owner could be in the EGLP for up to a maximum of eight years. The EGLP operates for eight years from the date of inception unless the partners want to extend the time.
- **Step 7** The owner receives a share of the EGLP net profit, and the rescued equity (capital invested) is returned in full.

JOINING IS A MUST

The Trust Deed Pledge Plan offers a property owner who cannot cure their foreclosure problem a one-of-a-kind way to solve the problem. The owner can now rescue their entire financial nest egg, which is represented by the equity in their property, that they are counting on for their future security.

PART 2
"TRUST DEED PLEDGE PLAN" (TDPP)
IN THE EQUITY GROWTH LIMITED PARTNERSHIP

A SPECIAL PLAN

The Equity Rescue's Trust Deed Pledge Plan is revolutionary. Not every real estate plan has so much to offer as the Equity Rescue's TDPP. By designing the TDPP to rescue equities from foreclosure to raise operating and investment capital in large amounts quickly, the plan is an original introduction! As a result of helping property owners avoid foreclosure and rescue their equity, the ability to build a new type of Operating & Investment Fund (O&IF) in a limited partnership becomes possible.

While helping owners with one of the most serious financial problems they have is most gratifying, the Equity Rescue Program's MAIN REASON is to earn profit by creating an investment Operating and Investment Fund (O&IF) in each EGLP started. By designing the TDPP to rescue equities from foreclosure to raise investment capital in large amounts quickly, the plan becomes an industry leader! Never has such an ability been developed to gather so much investment capital on a never-ending basis.

Financial problems that cannot be addressed without substantial reserve cash to ensure success can now be taken on and answered. A variety of new investment and financial opportunities are original and profitable because of the plan. The plan is a financial source for providing answers to many different real estate money problems.

The TDPP can raise millions of dollars of investment capital by helping property owners rescue their equity from foreclosure. The fund size will accumulate exponentially, allowing for extremely safe and rewarding investments to be formulated for the first time. When several individual EGLPs are operating, each can gather investment capital rapidly. The O&IF will garner investment capital forever because many foreclosures will occur each year forever. This powerful way to gather large sums of investment capital is a first-time achievement.

DRAMATIC INVESTMENT QUESTIONS

- How can a property owner, who cannot cure a pending foreclosure to avoid all the nasty financial consequences a foreclosure causes, arrange it? The TDPP is the only way to arrange for the owner a fair and honest financial answer.
- Where is a legally safe and secure investment found that pays a fixed minimum reward of $25,500 to a maximum of $42,500 in about a year, with no personal investor time or legal liability? This question exactly describes what the PCI receives in the TDPP.
- How are extraordinarily large sums of investment capital accumulated on a repetitive never-ending basis to safely invest in real estate ventures accomplished? The TDPP transaction will raise a large amount of investment capital, one amount at a time if there are foreclosures. This will create an EGLP O&IF that will grow quickly to use to invest in innovative ways. This is a first-time achievement.

PROFESSIONAL REAL ESTATE QUESTION

Suppose a real estate professional was asked from an owner of the property who cannot pay the money to cure an ongoing foreclosure. Can you help me avoid losing all my property equity built up over the years? The professional will have to answer; I am sorry if you cannot pay the default amount, I know of no way for you to save your property equity. Equity Rescue now changes the professional's answer *"yes, I know of a way"* Equity Rescue can rescue 100% of the equity for you, using the EGLP/TDPP.

Foreclosure is not only the owner's problem. It is also a societal problem. The process is unfair because the financial punishment is very severe. Loss of years of supporting the monthly property payments to build up the equity as a nest egg for retirement is a loss. Other nasty long-term financial consequences also badly hurt the property owner for years. There are many reasons a property owner can go into foreclosure. Loss of job suddenly, unexpected medical bills, and on and on. So, the point is sometimes the owner has not been financially acting irresponsibly. Outside forces are many times the cause of foreclosure. There is no way in the general market scenario to help the owner save all the remaining equity in the property. Equity Rescue does rescue all the equity for the owner! The Trust Deed Pledge Plan, a new real estate transaction, can perform the task.

NEW TECHNICAL ARRANGEMENT

The TDPP is a three-party real estate transaction between a property owner in foreclosure, a secured cash investor, and the EGLP. The EGLP has two types of limited partners. The foreclosure owner who contributes property to the EGLP that will act as collateral is called the "Equity Growth Partner" (EGP) or "owner". A secured investor is called the "Privilege Cash Investor" (PCI). The EGLP features two types of very different investors in the same Partnership, a PCI and a property owner in foreclosure that is turned into a cash investor. Each limited partner has an individual purpose and a different legal and investment position in the EGLP.

THE TDPP LOOKS LIKE BUT

The EGLP/TDPP legal structure is the major "most intricate and critical part" of the Equity Rescue Real Estate Transaction. It allows new investment and operational techniques that create a greatly improved ability to perform in a new way.

The TDPP is like a standard everyday looking real estate transaction in that there is a buyer, seller, and transfer of property when it is completed. However, there is a special challenge for the EGLP to solve a foreclosure that involves more than just doing a standard buy-sell transaction. An EGLP/TDPP general overview:

- The EGLP finds a qualified property in foreclosure.
- The investor approves the property to secure invested funds.
- The owner, cash investor, and EGLP enter into an agreement.
- The property is listed for sale and sold by the EGLP through a Broker.

The TDPP Looks like a regular transaction, doesn't it? However, the TDPP has a very different legal, financial, and investment structure and procedure. The structure in the TDPP has a different legal arrangement using existing legal statutes and regulations. Together in a "new formation," they allow for an original way to solve a serious foreclosure problem in a better and honest way! The grouping of these legal statutes in a new alinement is what creates a way to process a long sought-after solution.

UNIQUE ACHIEVEMENT

The EGLP/TDPP has a special challenge to solve a property foreclosure and rescue the owner's equity from loss to foreclosure. To accomplish this, it involves an original method of operating that is exclusive to the EGLP/TDPP. The legal structure and procedures are very different and operate in a profoundly original way. The EGLP/TDPP completely invents a unique capability to rescue property equity from foreclosure.

Within the TDPP, a new real estate financial approach enters the market. Its methods and operation have never existed before. Under severe financial duress, the owner is helped to become a qualified investor in a new exclusive arrangement. The entire equity in the property is rescued for the owners and grows with profit share while all the ugly consequences of a foreclosure are avoided. This answer is not found in any other investment arrangement and is truly a unique development that saves a financial catastrophe from occurring to the owner. All the professional time, talent, and use of the exclusive TDPP are cost-free to the property owner. The EGLP/TDPP addresses in a positive way a large segment of the foreclosure market that has never been approached before in a helpful way.

- The TDPP provides a financial answer to a large part of the foreclosure market and offers a new safe and rewarding secured way to invest.
- The Plan arranges financial benefits for property owners, real estate brokers, lenders, and related businesses never offered in any other investment.
- The social value is extensive as it is clearly a win-win for everyone involved, especially the property owners across the country. It also provides original substantial paying real estate job opportunities.
- There are several key elements of law used, and specially designed investment strategies introduced in the TDPP that establish a brand-new investment opportunity.
- It can raise large sums of investment capital that will provide answers for all kinds of real estate financing problems.
- Most of all it is an "original investment plan" for secured cash investors and financially troubled property owner investors. The risk-reward status created for both original types of investors is outstanding and sets a new standard for real estate investing.
- The market is not limited to just the foreclosure market. Equity Rescue's ability to raise large amounts of operating and investment capital for the EGLP to invest makes it possible to deal with a wide range of property owners' real estate financing problems.
- It is not every real estate transaction that has so much to offer as the TDPP.

ADVANCEMENTS ARE ACCOMPLISHED

The Deed of Trust Pledge Plan sequence has many salient points that are a part of the whole sequence of operation. The "Deed of Trust Pledge Plan" creates and provides the following first-time ever procedural arrangements in a limited partnership.

THEY ARE:

- A Deed of Trust Pledge is used to secure Partnership promises made to its limited partners and promises made through the partnership by the limited partners to each other. The Deed of Trust Pledge legally enforces the limited partner's contractual promises and the promises made by the limited partnership.
- A safe and legal way of advancing funds to cure a foreclosure on behalf of the owners when no other lender would lend to the owners and the owners could not pay the arrearage themselves.
- A limited partnership acts as a legal intermediary representing both partners to accomplish their individual personal needs and intentions inside the partnership.
- Using a legally established Deed of Trust Pledge in a new way to bring partners with different roles and responsibilities together in a partnership, to accomplish the needs, intentions, and desires of both limited partners.
- Legally establishing a new type of dual collateral concept in a partnership and creating a "priority use position" for one limited partner.
- Creating a very low investment risk factor for the investor that is not matched in other partnerships or real estate investments.

- Establishing a legal right to property title, not just an equity lien position, as collateral for invested capital in a partnership.
- Creating a legal pre-agreed fixed amount of bonus, as a new payment system, for rewarding one limited partner.
- Legally securing the early return of capital and bonus payment for just one limited partner in a Limited partnership.
- Making a non-qualified insolvent investor (property owner in foreclosure) into a legal qualified investor immediately upon joining a viable funded EGLP.
- An investment interaction ability between limited partnerships not found in other limited partnerships or real estate investment plans
- A new very quick legal collection method for the cash investor if the EGLP does not perform and pay the investor as promised.

TDPP PARTICULAR PERFORMANCE

The Trust Deed Pledge Plan (TDPP) is embedded in the Equity Growth Limited Partnership (EGLP). The EGLP using the TDPP creates a special legal, financial, and investment answer to rescuing property equities from foreclosure. However, the explicit purpose of the EGLP/TDPP is to raise many millions of operating and investment dollars.

The property owners taken out of foreclosure are made into investors in the EGLP by using the rescued equities as capital, to invest and earn a profit! It features an original property investment strategy in a partnership. There are financial benefits for both the property owner in foreclosure and a secured cash investor we call the "Privilege Cash Investor" (PCI). There will be several properties secured from the many owners who all will become investors by using their rescued equity in the EGLP.

The plan has original innovations:
- Creating an original Limited Partnership design for two types of limited partners who have different purposes and personal qualifications.
- Rescuing all the remaining equity in the owner's property from foreclosure solely for the property owner's benefit.
- Gathering large sums of partnership capital in an Operating and Investment Fund for investment that will grow exponentially in a never-before conceived method.
- Creating a specially designed safe and rewarding investor position with many legal and financial protections in a Limited Partnership.
- Securing with substantial collateral an investor's capital invested in a partnership.
- Investing safely to collect a pre-agreed fixed bonus amount as a reward.
- Earning personal income in new and exclusive ways for the partners and real estate licensees.
- Raising operating and investment capital in a profoundly new way.
- Rescuing equities from foreclosure loss.
- Creating an original way to solve all types of real estate financing problems.
- Providing a new money opportunity solution for various financially troubled properties.
- Establishing a different system for a property owner to invest in.
- Creating a new type of limited partnership with an original investment system.
- Identifying a new investment financing system.
- Original innovative real estate transactions come to light.

THE EGLP/TDPP HAS MANY ORIGINAL METHODS OF OPERATION
The TDPP Design:
- Legally enforces the limited partner's contractual promises made by the limited partnership.

- Is used to provide a safe and legal way of advancing funds to cure a foreclosure on behalf of the owners when the owners could not pay the arrearage themselves.
- Is used to legally establish a new way to bring two types of limited partners with different roles and responsibilities together in a limited partnership, to accomplish the needs, intentions, and desires of both limited partners.
- Is used to establish a new type of dual collateral concept in a partnership by creating a "Priority Use Position" (PUP) for the benefit of one limited partner investor.
- Is used to establish a second way in a partnership to be financially successful for an investor, creating a very low investment risk for the investor.
- Establishes a legal right to a fee property title, not just an equity lien position, as collateral for the invested capital in a partnership.
- Creates a legal pre-agreed fixed amount of bonus, as a new payment system, for rewarding one limited partner in a partnership.
- Creates a way to secure the early return of capital and bonus payment for just one limited partner in a partnership. It gives rise to a quick turnover system that rapidly increases the rate of return for the investor.
- Creates a way of making a non-qualified insolvent investor (property owner in foreclosure) into a qualified cash investor immediately upon joining the EGLP.
- Creates an investment interaction ability in a partnership not found in another partnership or real estate investment plan.
- Creates a new very quick legal collection method to collect the collateral for the cash investor.

EGLP/TDPP INVESTMENT ABILITIES ESTABLISHED
Here are innovative operational techniques in the EGLP/TDPP:
- A way for limited partners to participate in a cooperative solution was created
- A special form of Articles Of Partnership was created
- A tax-deferred capital contribution of the property was used
- A way to create a secured transaction in a limited partnership had to be created
- A system that created sufficient collateral is established
- A separation of limited partners by creating 2 classes of limited partners
- New use of a Performance Trust Deed was established
- A conditional grant deed transaction is created
- A way to gain title to property without paying for the property was created
- A new use for a bare title ownership status was established
- A new type of financial support plan was established to finance the plan
- A special legal position for a cash investor was established
- A full sale advantage for foreclosure property was created
- A default collection system for cash investors needed to be in place
- A new Debt to Asset formula needed to be established for a property with a money problem.

THE EGLP/TDPP "PERFORMANCE TRUST DEED" INVESTMENT
A NEW trust deed investment plan is born! It is called the "Trust Deed Pledge Plan" because it is a new way to invest in a secured trust deed investment. A "Performance Trust Deed" (PTD) is used in the TDPP versus a regular trust deed investment is eye-opening and financially enriching.

A PTD is a legal instrument that has the effect of securing a pledge of a property "fee ownership" with a rich equity position as collateral. The PTD is the legal position that secures the PCI funds invested in the

EGLP. The EGLP has a bare title, and the PCI receives a PTD from the EGLP and is recorded against the property. The safety, reward, and timing differences between regular trust deed investing and the PTD investment are significant for the investor!

Earning Improvement
Standard Deed of Trust Investment
Results vary in regular trust deed investing from single digit to double-digit returns. Potential negative variables occur that could cause a loss. The amount of return is unknown until completion.
Major Distinction
This new Trust Deed way offers a pre-agreed fixed amount of $25,500 up to $42,500 in approximately one year. The same potential negative variables in a regular trust deed investment are not possible in this PTD Investment.

Collateral Improvement
Standard Deed of Trust Investment
Only a share of the property equity protects the funds invested. If the owner does not pay the monthly payments the property equity total can diminish by the amount not paid very rapidly. And a foreclosure if started becomes a serious time, money, and legal problem for the investor.
Major Distinction
The collateral given to the investor in the TDPP exceeds by far the amount that a typical trust deed Investment offers. And loss that happens in regular trust deed investing is not possible in this trust deed structure because of the nature of the collateral agreement and the collection ability of the PCI.

Foreclosure/Bankruptcy Improvement
Standard Deed of Trust Investment
The borrower's nonpayment could create legal problems such as foreclosure or bankruptcy for the investor/lender. This is costly and time-consuming that could severely diminish the investor's return.
Major Distinction
In the TDPP PTD legal scenario, foreclosure or bankruptcy that would cost the investor time and money cannot happen to the PCI.

Investment Time Improvement
Standard Deed of Trust Investment
The average length of a loan secured by a trust deed is three to five years.
Major Distinction
PTD investment timing is approximately one (1) year or less in California. Note: The timing can be shortened even further with repeat investment and would also increase the amount of the investor's reward.

SEVERAL NEW AND ORIGINAL TECHNIQUES
Each occurrence listed below is a new real estate unique technical performance in a limited partnership! Together they offer outstanding investment protection and rewards for all the limited partners.

- The owner's pending foreclosure is cured using the TDPP that operates in the EGLP, in a profoundly new way!
- The TDPP arranges for the owner to rescue 100% of the property equity for the owner's sole benefit, without any expense for the help.
- The TDPP is unique in that several different owners contribute their property title to the EGLP without the EGLP paying for the property that will be sold by the EGLP.

- In the TDPP the EGLP secures collateral inside the EGLP with a conditional pledge of the property title made to the PCI.
- A Grant Deed is used in the TDPP to transfer a Bare Title for a new purpose and in a new way for the first time in a limited partnership.
- A Performance Trust Deed is used for a new reason and in a new way in the TDPP.
- A specially created bonus plan never designed or offered to a secured cash investor anywhere, in any legal entity of any type, is part of the TDPP.
- In the TDPP two classes of limited partners are established in the EGLP, each having different legal, financial, and investment roles in the EGLP, which separate roles have never been invented or used in a limited partnership before.
- One can ascertain insight into a new PCI Risk-Reward paradigm in the TDPP by reviewing the legal protection, financial reward, and investment status of the PCI that is second to none in other real estate investment endeavors!
- In the TDPP the PCI is secured within the EGLP with substantial collateral while all other EGLP limited partners are not secured and are at risk to the extent of the capital amount invested.

THE PLAN DOES A LOT FOR MANY
- Self-Generates Operating & Investment Capital
- Provides a Foreclosure Answer
- Answer for All Financially Troubled Property
- New Safety Technologies Incorporated
- New Exclusive Forms of Earnings
- New Transaction Designs and Opportunities for the Lender, Broker, and related businesses
- All types of properties qualify for the TDPP: Residential, Commercial, Apartments, Retail, Development projects, Land

SAFETY EVENTS
The TDPP offers the Privilege Cash Investor security advantages:
- Real Property fee title is the investors collateral.
- Two forms of security for the PCI; property title, EGLP cash reserves, and any loan payments made by the owner all act as funds to protect the PCI.
- The PCI enjoys a Priority Use Position (PUP) that protects the PCI funds invested in the EGLP.
- The cash-on-hand increases after the start of the investment with each property sale made by the EGLP and adds to the PCI security.

ACCOMPLISHED FOR MANY
The EGLP/TDPP does a lot:
- For society:
  Solves a serious and difficult foreclosure problem in a fair and just way that society has not been able to solve for centuries.
- For businesses:
  Saves money for lending institutions and other businesses in new ways. Listing and selling properties taken out of foreclosure for full value becomes possible for real estate brokers.
- For the PCI:
  Creates a better way to invest that is safer, more rewarding, and has a quicker turn-over rate then what is the average in other real estate investments.
- For investors improves safety:
  Creates a safer legal and financial vehicle for real estate investors

Creates a first-time method to increase investment collateral for a PCI

- For property owners:
  Cures legal and financial problems created by a notice of default.
  Gives the owners a fresh financial and emotional start.
  Creates a new investment method for the property owners.
- For the US government:
  Lower the number of bankruptcies cases and saves the government money.
  Creates jobs and tax income for the government in several ways
- For investing in general:
  The TDPP can raise large sums of investment capital that will provide answers to all kinds of real estate financing problems.
  Most of all it is an original investment plan for secured cash investors and financially troubled property owners.
  Creates a unique and safe way to completely fund a partnership.
  Affords an acceleration plan to increase the investment rate of return.
  The risk-reward status created for both original types of investors is outstanding and sets a new standard for real estate investing.
  The Equity Rescue Program's market is not limited to just the foreclosure market.

NO STOP DATE
The TDPP will be needed forever! When the following facts are understood it will come clear that the need of for the TDPP will go on forever.

1) The lender lending rules will never change! The institutional lenders such as banks and savings and loans will not as a rule loan on a property that has a Notice Of Default (NOD) recorded against it. Any loan from an equity lender must be protected.
2) No lender will lend money unless there is enough equity to cover the loan amount and cost to collect. The general rule is the equity lender will not lend money more than 70% Loan To Value.
3) Also, the lender lending this way must also qualify the borrower the same as an institutional lender does. THIS WILL NEVER CHANGE!

The Foreclosure Law Will Never Change!
The laws regarding foreclosure are geared to legally recover the collateral (property) in case the loan is defaulted upon. So, if the loan is defaulted upon the lender must foreclose and sell the property to collect the funds loaned. THIS WILL NEVER CHANGE!

Foreclosure Market Will Always Exist And Grow!
This is because the lenders who loan money do not have a crystal ball. The lender can review a loan application very carefully. However, they will never know what will happen to the borrower that will change his or her financial standing in a negative way as time goes on. This is the reason the lender's judgment is good only for a moment in time. This phenomenon is built into the process. THIS WILL NEVER CHANGE!

The Number Of Foreclosures!
The number of foreclosures will always grow because the number of new properties built that could go into foreclosure in the future. Also, there are a multiple of financial reasons why an owner of property cannot pay the loan payment that cause the default. With these reasons and the new amount of building that continually goes on one can see that there will forever be foreclosure occurring in the United States. THIS WILL NEVER CHANGE!

Human Nature Causes The Owner A Money Problem!
No person whether a qualified new buyer or a foreclosure profit speculator will pay the full fair market value of the property in the process of being foreclosed. Everyone purchasing property for whatever reason always offers the lowest price to purchase the property. In the case of a property in foreclosure the amount offered to the owner usually equals the loan value plus a few thousand dollars. THIS WILL NEVER CHANGE!

The Trust Deed Pledge Plan Is An Original And Exclusive Plan!
When one understands how the Trust Deed Pledge Plan works and what it does for the owner in foreclosure one could ask the question. What owner would refuse to participate in the plan? Just about no one would give up an opportunity to rescue all his or her hard-earned equity and make it grow in lieu of losing the equity. Refusing the offer to participate in the plan means that the owner would have to submit to a forced sale at a foreclosure auction or for a sale for pennies on the dollar to a profit speculator. THIS WILL NEVER CHANGE!

EVERYONES SAFE REWARDING INVESTMENT MODEL
A real estate investor is always looking for a great investment. An original investor great investment model is created. The Plan introduces an exceptionally safe and rewarding investment for a PCI. A unique investment structure in a Limited Partnership has been developed that is anchored in legal, financial, and investment principles that greatly protect and reward a PCI!

The PCI funds invested are highly collateralized using a new financial technique and a different legal design that establishes a strong and highly rewarding investment. The investor's capital is secured from the point of commitment to completion and there is no management or legal responsibility for the investor in the Plan. The investor is granted new and separate legal positions with major financial advantages that form a first-time investment innovation! The Plan is carefully designed to avoid any investor loss from happening.

TDPP achievement for "the owner". The desperate need for many thousands of property owners in America to avoid foreclosure and rescue all their property equity is answered. For the owner who cannot solve a pending foreclosure, the TDPP has been designed to help rescue the property equity from foreclosure. The TDPP cures the foreclosure, rescues the equity, and makes the owner into a qualified investor to grow the rescued equity. The special ability to rescue the equity and make it grow has never been designed before now.

People and government all benefit financially: The owner is helped a very great deal. The PCI has a safer and very rewarding investment. The Lender is very grateful to have the foreclosure cured and the principal paid. The Real Estate Broker is glad to have a non-foreclosure listing with time to sell. The individuals representing the Equity Rescue Program earn in exclusive ways. The Government collects a lot of tax money. The Investors outside the plan will have a new joint venture partner. The EGLP operates in a safe fashion and earns profit for all its partners.

FACTS ARE FACTS
It is dangerous to say never because someone is going to say that is not true. However, in the case of three major achievements created in the TDPP we can say they are unique and achieve very impressive results. So, we will say these are superior achievements that have "never been" designed, developed, instituted or equaled anywhere before without fear of contradiction!

The TDPP is organized and operates in a profoundly unique way. The innovative procedure has the same result of a normal property sale. However, it does much more because of what it achieves for the owner, cash investor and foreclosure market. The TDPP solves a large segment of the foreclosure market that has never been addressed before with success.

The TDPP has a very high social value because it solves many different financial problems for property owners, investors, lenders, the bankruptcy court, real estate professionals, and related businesses. The TDPP will create many new types of desirable jobs. It will provide new wealth for the owners, investors, and businesses in a better safer way.

There are no good options offered in the marketplace for an owner. The remedies offered in the marketplace for property in the foreclosure process are of no financial help to the owners. The owner can arrange a give-away-sale price and suffer the loss of the equity in the property. Or the owner's property is sold at a forced foreclosure auction that will cause the loss of the equity. The EGLP/TDPP is the only positive financial answer for the owner who cannot cure the pending foreclosure themselves.

PART 3
THE PRIVILEGE CASH INVESTOR (PCI)
IN THE EQUITY GROWTH LIMITED PARTNERSHIP

FINDING THE RIGHT INVESTMENT

A qualified investor is always looking for a great investment that is safe and rewarding just like the EGLP/TDPP offers the PCI. A unique investment structure in a Limited Partnership has been developed that is anchored in legal, financial, and investment principles that greatly protect and reward a PCI. The legal protection and collateral system combination originates a very attractive low-risk high-return advanced way for the PCI to invest, one that is very difficult to equal. The investment features a highly collateralized and secured investor position.

The PCI is a new type of "secured limited partner" investor in an EGLP that invests cash in the EGLP as a limited partner. The PCI has an innovative legal and very safe way for a PCI to let the EGLP use funds as operating capital. The PCI investment is revolutionary in original, innovative, and profound ways. It offers strong built-in legal, financial, and investment protections and benefits never arranged and offered to an investor anywhere. The EGLP/TDPP changes investing in foreclosure into a financially safe and highly rewarding PCI investment. The PCI has a groundbreaking strategic legal, financial, and investment structure incorporated in the EGLP, which is specially designed to create safety and reward for a PCI.

The concept of "investor privilege" is created to encourage financially capable investors to participate in an investment that involves curing an active foreclosure for the property owner. The PCI start-up investment funds allow the EGLP to begin operating. This investment by the PCI is what earns the PCI a handsome amount of bonus. The PCI is not involved in any EGLP investment for-profit project.

PCI HAS A SPECIAL LIMITED PARTNER POSITION

The PCI limited partner has his/her own individual limited partner legal, financial and investment position in the EGLP. The EGLP "legal structure" has been designed and arranged so that the owners and the PCI have different rights, obligations, timing, and methods of reward. The two different classes of investors do not depend upon any performance or promise of each other. Two very different types of investment opportunities have been created in the same limited partnership. This arrangement safeguards and eliminates any legal, financial, or investment entanglement of any kind for the PCI with other limited partners.

THE PCI's ROLE

What does the "Privilege Cash Investor" do in the EGLP? The PCI is a limited partner investor in name only, as the PCI does not participate in an investment for the profit of the EGLP of any kind. The PCI is only investing start-up funds that are secured with "a pledge" of fee ownership of property approved by the PCI. The property taken out of foreclosure by the EGLP is the collateral pledged to secure the start-up funds. The EGLP/TDPP using the PCI funds invested will afford owners in dire need of financial help, a fair and honest answer to their foreclosure problem. The PCI invests EGLP start-up funds in return for a healthy reward in the form of a hefty bonus. The one act the PCI has is to invest capital to financially prime the start-up of an EGLP.

THE PCI INVESTMENT QUESTIONS & ANSWERS

The PCI's reason for investing is to earn an attractive return in a low-risk investment in the shortest time with the fewest problems possible. This statement describes what happens for the PCI in the EGLP.

Investing in this original way affords the PCI a very safe investment with a large reward, for helping others solve a pending foreclosure. The desire to be protected in a safe rewarding and timely investment is what the investor wants and needs. The PCI investment does this, here are the details:

- What is the minimum investment amount required?
  Ans: $60,000 by a group of investors or a single amount of $60,000.
- What is the reward?
  Ans: Pre-agreed amount of $25,500 up to $42,500.
- What is the timing of investment?
  Ans: Estimated one year.
- What is the collateral/security?
  Ans: Equity-rich property "fee ownership "chosen by the PCI is the collateral.
- What is the amount of protection?
  Ans: Collateral exceeds invested amount. Superior legal standing.
- What is the investment for profit project required?
  Ans: No profit investment is required by the EGLP to pay the investor
- What is the source of the PCI reward?
  Ans: The reward is initially paid out of a foreclosure property sale. Then the EGLP replaces the bonus money out of profit earned. The owner does not pay the PCI.
- What is the reinvestment opportunity?
  Ans: It is a good one, the reward increases substantially.
- What is the Investor personal time required?
  Ans: No investor legal, management, or responsibility.
- Who is the Equity Rescue manager?
  Ans: A Real Estate Company

INVESTMENT CONCERN

Question? Would anyone become an investment partner with a financially insolvent property owner whose property is in foreclosure? Under no circumstance would a financially qualified investor be willing to invest cash and become a partner with a financially insolvent property owner. Unless all the investor concerns in this regard can be eliminated by keeping the two partners' legal, financial, and investment positions separated as is the case in the EGLP.

ADDRESSING THE PCI CONCERNS

To attract a PCI to fund the start-up of an EGLP, the PCI needs to be financially favored and legally protected as much as possible. So, how is the PCI attracted to invest? A set of unprecedented safe and legal protections along with first-time investment advantages and a substantial reward is granted to the PCI, this makes the investment extremely attractive from every investment aspect.

The "Articles of Partnership" agreement and the "Performance Trust Deed" gives the PCI two separate legal standings in the same investment. Other legal and financial advantages are given, and superior precautions are taken in the EGLP for the PCI. The EGLP safeguards established for the PCI equal unprecedented protection and create a desirable safe and rewarding way to invest. A legal structure has been designed to ensure the PCI concerns are met as follows:

- The PCI needs must be kept legally and financially "separated" in every way to distinguish and protect the PCI from all the other EGP limited partners that join the EGLP. The EGLP structure does this by creating two classes of limited partners in the EGLP.
- The PCI needs to be "secured" at all times in such a manner that the PCI knows that the return of the funds invested is made and the bonus payment is paid by the EGLP. The PCI will not sign off

the Performance Trust Deed securing the collateral if all terms and conditions agreed to in the Articles are not completed as promised.

- The PCI needs to be "paid" on a different basis than all the other partners. The PCI is paid with a pre-agreed fixed amount of bonus, paid out of EGLP property sales. Using property sale income to first pay and then replace the amount used from EGLP profit does this.
- The PCI must be and is "favored" with many legal, financial, and investment advantages. The PCI investment is featured with first-time protections never designed in one investment. The PCI is greatly favored in the EGLP.
- The PCI investment funds must be and are "financially separated" in the EGLP to verify use of the funds. This accounting of funds protects the PCI from misuse and makes the EGLP accountable. The PTD sign-off also controls the use of the funds going to the next property. This accounting has been set up in the Articles to protect the PCI fund.
- The PCI must be and is assured that the EGP limited partners have "no decision-making ability" in the EGLP. The legal structure of a limited partnership requires this. This is automatic in a limited partnership by law and is the case in the EGLP.
- The PCI must be in and out of the investment as quickly as possible. The "estimated time" for the PCI to collect the bonus and leave the EGLP is one year. All other limited partners must stay in the EGLP until it dissolves. This is the EGLP legal structure agreed to in the EGLP Articles.
- The PCI must not have and does not have any participation in any EGLP "management or legal responsibility" in the EGLP. The PCI simply does nothing but waits for three properties to be taken into the EGLP and sold. Participation is not allowed for any limited partner in the EGLP.

PCI LEGAL SAFETY INNOVATIONS

- Fee ownership of a property with substantial equity approved by the PCI is the PCI collateral.
- A Performance Trust Deed secures PCI legal rights and collateral made to the PCI in the EGLP.
- The PCI is safe financially because of two separate categories of collateral (cash and property) that act as security for the PCI.
- The legal and reward aspects arranged for the PCI create an attractive investment position.
- Secured capital is arranged at the start and the PCI is always secured from start to finish.
- The PCI has the right to approve the first EGLP property as collateral. Simply put the investor is naming the amount of collateral that the investment will provide by approving a property.
- The cash from property sales adds to the collateral position of the PCI because of the Priority Use Position (PUP).
- A PCI legal, financial, and investment position defines a new degree of protection and safety for the PCI. The PCI has two separate legal positions (the Articles and the PTD) that are dual legal standings for the PCI to collect collateral.
- A special individual class of limited partner position is arranged separating the PCI from the other property owner limited partners in every way.
- No foreclosure or bankruptcy concern or expense can affect the PCI. It is not possible for the PCI to be involved in a bankruptcy or foreclosure.

PCI OPERATIONAL ADVANTAGES

Overseeing spending by the EGLP. The PCI funds invested must be spent on only allowed EGLP expenditures:

- To immediately cure the subject property foreclosure, to prepare the property for sale by the EGLP, to pay any escrow closing costs to transfer the title to the EGLP, to support the monthly loan(s) payments on the property, if necessary.

- No cash reserves are required for the investor to back up invested funds. The investor funds invested have limited use and if they are exhausted without a property sale, the collateral is given over to the PCI automatically.
- PCI's pre-agreed fixed amount of bonus money is agreed to at the very start of the investment. The PCI does not depend on any profit venture being successful for the EGLP to pay the bonus.
- The Bonus is safer and quicker in each EGLP reinvestment made by the PCI. The time for the PCI to collect is approximately one year.
- There is a pre-agreed fixed reward limit of $42,500 in any one EGLP.
- PCI knows the property will be up for sale immediately. Why because the Articles dictate that the property must be offered for sale immediately.
- The owner will leave the property upon sale when asked. The owner wants to complete the transaction with all the equity rescued. A penalty for not moving on time would lower the rescued amount by several thousand dollars.
- No maintenance problem. Again, the owner wants the best price as is the usual case. Keeping the property in top condition is what will bring the best price.

LEGAL SAFETY

The legal standing for the PCI arranged in the EGLP/TDPP is exceptional in several ways:

- The PCI is given special legal promises that afford maximum protection in the EGLP. Dual legal standing positions are created for the PCI.
- The Articles of Partnership is a legally binding contract with terms and conditions that favor the PCI'S position. Also, the PCI receives a Performance Trust Deed that is a legal standing outside of the EGLP.
- The EGLP Articles of Partnership controls what the PCI investment capital is used for and confirms restricted use and that it must be replenished after each EGLP property sale. The PTD gives control of collateral collection in case of an EGLP default. These two, first-time-ever, separate PCI legal contractual standings solidify the investment standing for the PCI.
- The EGLP DAR formula (Debt to Asset Ratio) creates financial safety for the PCI.
- Property fee ownership goes to PCI if invested funds are exhausted without a property sale.
- The PCI is favored with many original legal, financial, and investment arrangements and Privileges.

ORIGINAL FINANCIAL SAFETY FEATURES

- There is a pre-agreed fixed reward limit of $42,500 in any one EGLP.
- Financial support plan (allows time for the EGLP to perform property sale).
- No bankruptcy or foreclosure concern for the PCI.
- Pre-agreed fixed amount of bonus agreed to insure the large return
- Payment of bonus and return of PCI capital paid directly from escrow.
- Payment of bonus and return of the investment fund is controlled by the PTD.
- Payment of bonus is not dependent on EGLP making a profit.
- PCI has a pre-agreed fixed amount of bonus that cannot go down.
- Return of capital and bonus payment dependent only on the sale of the property.
- No PCI cash reserve is required ever to protect the original amount invested.
- Three professional reports on the first EGLP property (appraisal, contractor, and prelim report).
- New debt to asset ratio creates liquidity and investor safety.

- The bonus plan in the EGLP TDPP is instituted for the very first time anywhere, allows the PCI to accelerate the bonus amount by turning over the funds from the last EGLP to the next EGLP. The rate of return and safety that is created by this method is outstanding.

NEW PCI SECURITY ARRANGEMENT
The EGLP/TDPP provides:
- Created a way for the PCI to pick and approve a property as collateral.
- A way to secure the collateral with a property title, not just the equity,
- A way to create dual collateral by including all EGLP cash as collateral,
- A method of increasing the collateral through partnership sales,
- A way for the PCI to check the financial activity of the EGLP,
- A way for the PCI to check the status of the EGLP collateral,
- A way for the PCI to be paid as agreed and on time.
- A way for the PCI to verify the status of the EGLP collateral at any time.

THE PCI IS PROVIDED MANY STRONG POSITIONS!
There are several strong advantages:
- A new financing advantage
- A new legal advantage
- A new safety advantage
- A new cash investor reward advantage
- A new timing advantage
- A new acceleration advantage
- A new investment advantage

THE PCI'S SUPERIOR INNOVATIVE ADVANTAGES
- A way for the PCI to be paid as agreed and on time. (See PCI section)
- The PCI has a separate limited partner class structure
- The Equity Rescue Debt to Asset Ratio low-risk structure
- The pledge of the property acts as a security structure
- The five legal positions combination structure
- The use of the PCI invested fund structure
- The bonus reward system structure
- The bonus reward collection structure
- The bonus timing structure
- The dual chances of success structure
- The dual PTD and Articles legal standing structure
- The dual collateral structure
- The system to increase the collateral structure
- The bankruptcy and foreclosure avoidance structure
- The normal partnership pitfalls avoidance structure
- The investment risk-reward structure

EVERY FIRST-TIME INVESTOR BENEFITS ESTABLISHED
New investment arrangements for the PCI:
- Created a way for the investor to pick and approve a property as collateral
- Created collateral increase system

- Created a special bonus plan
- Created bonus acceleration plan
- Created a way to secure only one limited partner
- Created very-low risk investment
- Created a secured pledge of property to secure the PCI
- Created a transfer of title transaction without paying for the property
- Created bonus collection system for cash investor
- Created a new risk-reward paradigm

PCI INVESTMENT FACTORS

Security Plus: An original way to use a Performance Trust Deed in a limited partnership for the first time is arranged. Securing an investor's collateral is critical along with a way to collect without involving the investor in a bankruptcy or foreclosure proceeding, in case of a default. This is of paramount importance for the investor. The TDPP provides the investor with a very positive answer that deals with and solves this concern.

Loan service: The EGLP will service the debt when the owner cannot pay. Cash reserves are planned to make this happen. The property cannot go back into foreclosure because of non-payment of the loan before it is sold.

Legal standing: There are legal positions that make the PCI legal standing very strong to collect the collateral if necessary.

Control of investment: Control of funds and debt service payments are the EGLP control.

Watching the EGLP expenditure: The PCI can verify the use of funds invested by the PCI through the restrictions laid down in the AP of what the PCI funds can be used for.

The property title: The PCI acquires the title automatically from the EGLP when the PCI funds are exhausted without a property sale occurring.

Agreement to sell: The PCI will see the property immediately put up for sale by the EGLP, as agreed in the AP.

Investment period: The estimated time for the investor to participate is one year. Typically, other real estate investments take many years to complete.

Investment payoff: The PCI is paid a pre-agreed, fixed amount of 42.5% of invested capital as a bonus. The payoff occurs when the third property is sold by the EGLP.

Security: EGLP cash and property fee ownership are both pledged and are used to secure the funds. The security increases with additional property sales by the EGLP.

Avoidance of potential problems: The possibility of a foreclosure or bankruptcy interfering with the collection of the collateral does not exist in the TDPP.

Acceleration opportunity: The estimated one-year time allows for repeat opportunities and increased security and lower risk. The PCI can have multiple investments working simultaneously.

<u>Property maintenance:</u> There is a lot to gain financially by improving and keeping up the property listed for sale in good condition as this motivates the owner so that the property can sell at full value.

KEY INDIVIDUAL HAPPENINGS

PROPERTY AS COLLATERAL

The amount of initial collateral is established by the PCI approving a property with substantial equity that will act as the collateral. Establishing a legal right to property ownership title, not just an equity lien position, as collateral for the PCI is created. The PCI in the EGLP has a substantial dual collateral arrangement. The collateral amount increases as the investment progress with each EGLP property sale that happens. The PCI security goes up because of the Priority Use Position that requires all EGLP cash on hand to be used before PCI funds can be expended. The risk goes down with each EGLP operating cash fusion due to a property sale.

THE SPECIAL PCI BONUS REWARD

The PCI receives a flat 42.5% of the amount invested as a bonus for providing start-up funds for the EGLP. The EGLP has a different way to pay the PCI with a pre-agreed bonus amount. The bonus can be a minimum of $25,500 to a maximum of $42,500. The bonus can increase to a maximum of $42,500 by reinvesting the first bonus earned into a new EGLP start-up. A small investment amount by each member in a group or a minimum of $60,000 up to $100,000 in a single amount can be invested.

The 42.5% is not an interest rate or rate of return, it is a lump sum bonus payment for a one-time act of providing start-up funds (seed money) to the EGLP. The time for the PCI to collect the bonus is approximately one year.

There is no dependence on the EGLP having to earn profit to pay the bonus. The Bonus is paid out of funds from the owner's property sales sold by the EGLP. The EGLP then refunds the bonus paid by the EGLP out of EGLP investment profits. The EGLP is paying the $25,500 PCI bonus for the owner with a credit back to the owner's capital account.

Within the TDPP a new method, the use of a PTD, to ensure the payment promised to the PCI is established. The PTD also ensures the return of the PCI investment capital along with the financial bonus promised. The PCI pre-agreed bonus is earned in an extraordinarily safe way by the PCI! The low-risk and high-return investment combination adds up to be very attractive, one that would be very difficult to equal.

PRIORITY USE POSITION

Increasing starting collateral:
A "Priority Use Position" (PUP) is granted to the PCI in the AOP. The "Priority Use Position" establishes a new type of dual collateral concept in a limited partnership to advantage the cash investor partner. The PCI A PCI has two types of financial safety positions in the EGLP because of the PUP.

First the PUP establishes that all the EGLP cash on hand must be spent before any PCI funds invested is spent. This means after the first property sale proceeds come into the EGLP, some or all the PCI funds will now be in reserve for the next property acquisition. As the initial PCI amount of investment funds have been replenished the added reserve position makes the investment safer for the PCI. The other collateral position for the PCI is the property pledge of fee ownership in the case that the PCI funds are exhausted without a sale of the property being made.

EGLP DEBT TO RATIO

The Debt to Asset Ratio (DAR) is changed by the cash amount invested from the PCI, the cash changes and improves the DAR. The Equity Rescue DAR creates a financial position that lowers and makes the investment risk factor acceptable. The percent of security goes up and the risk percentage goes down for the PCI in the TDPP. The PCI can invest safely and the EGLP can operate safely with the increase in cash. Advantages with the cash invested by the PCI:

- The PCI approves the property that will act as collateral and the Partnership cash on hand from each property sale also acts as additional collateral so the collateral increases with each property sale. This is because the PCI has a "Priority Use Position" on EGLP cash, all EGLP cash must be used before the PCI fund is used for any purpose.
- The collateral, the property equity amount is known at the start though the appraisal and is higher than the amount of the PCI capital invested. If it were not so the PCI would not make the investment and would not approve the property as collateral.
- The investor collateral collection of the property fee simple ownership cannot be stalled or involved in a foreclosure or bankruptcy. It is automatic according to the terms in the Articles of Partnership.
- There is a pre-agreed fixed reward limit of $42,500 in any one EGLP. The added cash makes the investment acceptable for the PCI. Taking property out of foreclosure with the PCI cash changes a duress sale into a full-price sale for the owner. For the PCI means a foreclosure-free property fee ownership becomes the collateral. Very importantly the cash allows for time to sell the property for full value.
- The PCI investment money is replenished after each EGLP property sale before a new property is taken into the EGLP. This creates a financial liquidity position that lowers the investor risk and makes the investment acceptable.

FINANCIAL SUPPORT PLAN

The money invested by the PCI creates a "financial support plan" in the EGLP. The PCI funds are given over, on a secured basis to the EGLP to cure a pending foreclosure on the property. Curing the pending foreclosure restores the property's full market value that will act as collateral. We call the PCI invested funds "Critical Cash Capital" (CCC). The CCC fund may be used by the EGLP to financially support the loan payments on the property until it sells. PCI cash invested protects the property from going back into foreclosure by paying mortgage payments, if necessary. The liquidity created by the PCI cash and the owners making the monthly payment (to the degree they can) is key financial supporting ingredients. This loan payment system maintains and solidifies the full equity position of the property until it is sold.

PCI MONEY POINTS

A Priority Use Position makes it a requirement that the EGLP uses all its cash on hand before any of the PCI fund money is used. This means the risk for the PCI is less because the EGLP is lowering the drawdown of the amount invested. The owner will pay the loan payments to the extent that is possible.

A Financial Support Plan using the PCI invested funds to support the property monthly loan payments is possible, if necessary. This will keep the property out of foreclosure until a sale occurs.

The $60,000 invested by the PCI has an expense spending limitation on items that it can be used for in the EGLP Articles of Partnership. It states clearly that the PCI funds cannot be used by the EGLP as venture capital or invested for profit. A separate EGLP accounting to ensure proper use of PCI funds is made for the PCI to review.

The only allowed EGLP expenditures of the PCI funds invested are:
- Created collateral increase system.
- To immediately cure the subject property foreclosure.
- To prepare the property for sale by the EGLP.
- To pay any escrow closing costs to transfer the title to the EGLP.
- To support the monthly loan(s) payments on the property, if necessary.
- To pay some EGLP operating expenses.
- All monies spent are replenished after each EGLP property sale.

THREE PROFESSIONAL REPORTS
Professional reports are used to analyze and approve the first property going into the EGLP. The investor approval or rejection is based on three professional reports plus a visit to the property if desired. A property appraisal, construction review report, and the Preliminary Title Report are provided to the PCI to make the decision. The following information is given to the PCI so that the PCI can make an informed decision, as to whether to approve the property as collateral? No investor approval means no commitment to invest.

The location will be determined by the PCI. Some locations are better than others and the PCI can review the desirability of the neighborhood offered for the PCI'S consideration. The appraisal will help in this regard. The amount of collateral/security can be estimated. An amount of net equity greater than the PCI funds and the amount of bonus added together, would be a good guideline to qualify the property as collateral.

PCI LOSS ISSUE
PCI is insulated. In a limited partnership, it is a fact that the limited partner is limited to losing only the amount invested by law. In the case of the PCI loss of capital, the PCI takes fee ownership of property offered as collateral that has substantial equity. The EGLP is required to pass the title of ownership to the PCI if the PCI funds are exhausted without a property sale occurring.

There would be no reason for the EGLP to not turn over the title to the PCI. There is no foreclosure or bankruptcy possible for the PCI to be involved in that would stall the collection of the collateral. The cash investor has two separate legal documents to exercise the collection of the collateral pledged, the Articles of Partnership and the Performance Trust Deed. Both have legal standing to collect.

LOAN IS SIMILAR
While the PCI investment is like making a "loan" to the EGLP it is not a loan. The PCI funds are invested as a limited partner (not loaned to the EGLP) in return for a pre-agreed fixed Bonus payment. No loan is "assumed" or "taken subject to" or applied for by the EGLP in the TDPP transaction. There is no requirement or need for the EGLP to take out a loan or become responsible for an existing loan in the TDPP.

"PERFORMANCE TRUST DEED" PERFORMS IN A NEW WAY
An original way to use a Performance Trust Deed in a limited partnership for the first time is arranged. Securing an investor's collateral is critical along with a way to collect it if the investment fails, without involving the investor in a bankruptcy or foreclosure proceeding. This is of paramount

importance for the investor. The TDPP provides the investor a very positive answer that deals with and solves this concern.

On each of the three properties taken into the EGLP, the PCI will receive a PTD as they are acquired. The first owner property is sold by the EGLP and any monies used out of the PCI invested funds to cure the foreclosure are replenished from sale proceeds. The PCI fund is replenished out of each EGLP property sale made for the owner. The second and third properties are acquired and sold by the EGLP in the same way. A pre-agreed Bonus amount is paid to the PCI at the time of the third EGLP property sale. The PCI is paid the bonus and leaves the EGLP at the time of the third property sale.

PCI COMMITMENT PROCESS

When does the PCI make a commitment? The PCI signs a letter saying he/she will invest $60,000 or more if and only if the PCI approves the property that will act as collateral to secure the PCI capital. The purpose of the letter is to show the owner that there is an investor with knowledge of the EGLP workings that is willing to invest. However, the investor's condition is that he/she approves the property that will act as collateral before agreeing to invest.

Commitment Point: After the approval of the property then the PCI goes to escrow and joins the Partnership with the owner and EGLP General Partner. The signing of the Articles of Partnership is the investor's investment commitment point. The PCI deposits the investment funds directly into escrow after joining the EGLP at the approbate time. Note: The property owner never receives or controls any of the funds invested by the PCI.

FAVORABLE PCI POINTS

- There is no legal or management responsibility for the PCI.
- The PCI timely real estate investment is approximately one year.
- The PCI will never be involved in any bankruptcy or foreclosure of the property with the TDPP collection system is designed to give over the collateral in case of a default.
- The investment is expense-free for the PCI.
- The Bonus is initially paid to the PCI out of EGLP property sales and reimbursed out of EGLP gross profits.
- The owner does not pay a dime for the help of money provided.

PCI ACTION

- The PCI makes an investment in the EGLP that is secured with a property that is taken out of foreclosure by the EGLP.
- The PCI will pick and approve a property that will have an equity amount greater than the amount invested plus the bonus promised.
- The PCI funds are never without collateral as the Bare Title is deposited into escrow before the PCI deposits funds.
- A Performance Trust Deed (PTD) secures a conditional pledge of property fee ownership to the PCI. The PCI is always in a secured investment from the ever start.

PCI EVENTS

- A secured pledge of PCI-approved collateral in the EGLP.
- A pledge of property fee ownership is the collateral, not just a lien against the equity position.
- A limited partnership cash and property ownership act together as collateral, creating a dual collateral system within a limited partnership.

- A financial plan maintains and increases the equity position with EGLP property sales.
- A PCI has a better legal system compared to other investments, to collect the collateral.
- A new Priority Use Position defines the first use of the EGLP capital and protects the PCI, creating special accounting requirements for all capital expended.

OVERVIEW OF A PCI INVESTMENT POSITION
- Equity Rescue DAR (Debt to Asset Ratio) creates investor safety.
- Three professional reports on properties provides necessary information.
- Do not have to risk investor capital in a risky partnership for profitable investment.
- Separate account is created for inspection to confirm EGLP PCI fund restricted use.
- Pre-agreed bonus amount is earned immediately upon joining.
- Investor early return of funds with bonus allows for reinvestment increased bonuses.
- No request for additional capital will be required to protect the original PCI funds.
- No bankruptcy or foreclosure is possible for the PCI to be involved in.
- Pre-agreed fixed amount of bonus agreed to at the start of the EGLP.
- Payment of bonus is dependent only on the sale of properties.
- The owner will leave the property when asked.
- No maintenance problem.
- Controlled spending.
- Contractual control of property ownership if PCI fund is exhausted by the EGLP.
- Performance is assured by the Performance Trust Deed given to the PCI.
- A sale of three appraised properties is all the investor is investing in.

Investment statement: No investor status has ever been devised that allows an investor to invest safely in a way that helps an owner in foreclosure to rescue all their property equity for themselves until Equity Rescue. The list above is a combination of newly generated factors in a limited partnership that, when put together, create a unique and safe way for the investor to participate in helping people rescue their equity. The PCI investment is safe and earns a substantial reward at the same time.

All legal and management responsibilities fall on the General Partner. A Low-risk high-return is what the PCI receives with the legal and reward system designed in the EGLP. The legal structure for the PCI is the strongest possible form of a risk-reward position for a real estate investor in a limited partnership. The way the TDPP brings the owner together with the PCI in the EGLP, in the same investment, is safe and is highly beneficial to both. The investment position granted to the PCI makes the investment a one-of-a-kind opportunity.

INFORMATION TO MAKE A DECISION TO INVEST
- Equity rescue's new debt to asset ratio creates investor safety.
- Three professional reports on properties.
- Do not have to risk investor capital in a partnership investment.
- Separate account open for inspection to confirm restricted use.
- Pre-agreed bonus amount is earned and secured immediately.
- Investor early return of capital accelerates earnings.
- No cash reserves are required to protect the original PCI investment.
- Favored with special investment privileges over all other partners.
- No bankruptcy or foreclosure concern for the PCI.
- Pre-agreed fixed amount of bonus means a large rate of return.

- Payment of bonus is not dependent on making a profit.
- Expense-free investment for the PCI.
- Contractual control of property ownership if PCI fund is exhausted.
- Payment of bonus and return of capital is controlled by the PTD.

ORIGINAL TECHNIQUES FOR THE PCI
PCI favorable investment overview:
- Quick timing
- Secured capital
- Pre-agreed fixed amount of bonus
- Dual collateral for security
- Security increase
- Two ways to be successful in one investment
- EGLP sales pay the PCI bonus for the owner
- Easy collection system
- Investment acceleration plan.

PCI POINT ADVANTAGES CONDENSED
- Secured investment with substantial collateral.
- Dual collateral that increases with property sales.
- No Involvement or Reliance on a Profit being made.
- Limited Use of Investor Fund.
- Bonus Pre-agreed and Secured.
- Bonus Paid from Existing Equities.
- Bonus Acceleration Plan.
- Short Time for a Real Return.
- No Limited Partnership Concerns.

PCI TRANSACTION BENEFITS
- No Limited Partnership Concerns.
- A very safe, quick, and rewarding investment.
- A low-risk high-return PCI position.
- Original legal, financial and investment structures.
- A unique PCI bonus payment system.
- A unique system to collateralize and secure the PCI.

TDPP INVESTMENT OPERATION
The TDPP original scenario in the EGLP creates a very safe, rewarding and timely PCI investment. The property in foreclosure is taken into escrow and cured by escrow. It is then listed for sale with a qualified broker. As far as the PCI is concerned it is a simple property listed, and property sold transaction completed by a real estate professional! How the TDPP is more involved legally and financially than the normal property sale transaction is detailed in the "EGLP section".

With the two separate EGLP/TDPP legal standings, the Performance Trust Deed and the Article of the Partnership agreement, and the fee ownership of property approved by the PCI acting as collateral an extremely safe PCI investment position is created. The PCI invests, on a secured basis in the "sale of properties" by real estate brokers, nothing else.

The new way of combining EGLP cash with a pledge of "out of foreclosure property ownership" as collateral makes the PCI investment very safe. EGLP money coming in from foreclosure rescued property sales cause the EGLP cash on hand to increase, which must be used first before any PCI funds are used. A Priority Use Position (PUP) for the PCI invested funds is created with an oversight confirmation capability to verify EGLP expenditures. This selling of properties taken out of foreclosure increases the EGLP operating cash and lowers the PCI risk.

The Debt to Asset Ratio (DAR). The PCI cash amount invested changes the DAR. The amount of PCI cash invested when added to the property value creates a higher total of assets at the very start of the EGLP. The property debt (loan amount) remains the same. With the cash invested by the PCI the EGLP can financially operate safely with the necessary amount of operating cash.

When the equity is rescued, the owner becomes an investor with the rescued equity. As more properties are sold it increases the EGLP operating fund balance, so the PCI risk goes down. This is because of the Priority Use Position that says all EGLP cash on hand must be used before the PCI fund money is used. A special account to keep track of the use of the PCI fund money must and is kept in a separate account for the PCI inspection.

OUTLINE TO BECOME A PCI LIMITED PARTNER IN AN EGLP
Safely designed avenue to become a PCI:

- The PCI reviews a "Preliminary Understanding" writing that is not a legal contract. The writing just explains how the TDPP works and spells out the terms, conditions, and roles for each limited partner in the Articles of Partnership. With this PCI Preliminary Understanding writing in hand the broker then locates a property in foreclosure for the PCI to approve.
- Three professional reports that deal with the property appraised value, physical condition and legal status is present to the potential investor for review.
- The PCI approves the first property that will act as collateral for the PCI funds invested. The PCI is the one deciding that the property will be good and sufficient collateral. The PCI will not invest unless the invested funds are secured with a property that has enough collateral (equity) approved by the PCI.
- The PCI then signs the EGLP Articles of Partnership after the owner signs and the PCI becomes a limited partner in the EGLP. The Articles are a legally binding agreement and are a blueprint for all partners.
- The PCI then deposits the investment funds directly into escrow after the escrow receives the Bare Title to property for the EGLP from the owner. The PCI will not give over any money to the escrow without the collateral security in place! The escrow company cures the Notice of Default on the property chosen by the PCI and the property is no longer in foreclosure.
- The PCI receives a Performance Trust Deed from the EGLP that is recorded against the property taken out of foreclosure to secure the funds invested. The value of the property becomes market value again as the property is no longer in foreclosure and subject to low offers.
- The PCI is now a secured investor with the pledge of the property ownership as collateral.
- Then with the PCI cash invested, the EGLP takes in a total of three properties in foreclosure, one at a time, and sells them through a qualified broker.
- The PCI signs off the first property Performance Trust Deed at closing and will receive a Performance Trust Deed on second property taken into the EGLP.
- The PCI waits for each property to sell to re-convey the PTD one at a time.
- When signing off the Performance Trust Deed on the third property sold, the PCI collects back the capital Invested along with the Bonus promised by the EGLP.

- The PCI's entire role in the TDPP is receiving and then re-conveying the PTD when each EGLP sale is made. Note: After each of the first two property sales the money used from the PCI money invested will be replenished to the full amount of the PCI fund, out of the sale proceeds. Each property taken in will have the full amount of PCI invested funds available to take in and sell each property.
- The money used from the property sales by the EGLP to pay the bonus ($25,500) is replenished from the gross profit earned by the EGLP. The owner's capital account will be credited with the $25,500 the EGLP used to pay the bonus.

PCI IS THE BEST INVESTMENT

The PCI in the EGLP is the most protected and rewarded investor in any Limited Partnership ever! Bold statement, however, is true when comparing it to any partnership investment standard. There never has been an investment in real estate in which an investor has been granted so many investment protections and advantages. A close review of all the legal, financial, and investment safeguards and advantages granted to the PCI will convince the most skeptical person that it is true! These privileged positions together create a safe, secured, strong, and high timely investment position for the PCI.

PART 4
EQUITY GROWTH LIMITED PARTNERSHIP (EGLP)©

EGLP NAMES AND POSITIONS
The legal entity for the Trust Deed Pledge Plan (TDPP) is the EGLP and the General Partner of the EGLP is a Corporation. There are fifty-plus EGLP Articles of Partnership. The EGLP has two types of limited partners, each has a special need and purpose for achievement. The owner who contributes property to the EGLP, which is in the foreclosure process, is called the "Equity Growth Partner" (EGP) or owner. The secured cash investor in the EGLP is called the "Privilege Cash Investor" (PCI). The EGLP features two legally organized and separate types of very different limited partner investors in the same Partnership. Each partner has a separate individual purpose and a different legal and investment position in the EGLP.

THE EGLP/TDPP DESCRIPTION
An original and exclusive EGLP is the legal agreement between limited partners expressing the terms and conditions of the partners. Within the EGLP there operates an original real estate transaction called the "Trust Deed Pledge Plan" (TDPP). The construct and intent of the EGLP/TDPP together are unique and pronounce a new way to operate to achieve special purposes. The legal, finance, and investment individual design of the EGLP and the TDPP are new discoveries. The benefits for the lender, property owner, PCI, real estate community, and the US government are superior to any other limited partnership or real estate investment design, in many ways. Investing in foreclosure and any other financially troubled real estate property just became safe and profitable.

ANSWERS FOR TWO TYPES OF INVESTORS
The EGLP addresses both an investment improvement and a property owner's foreclosure problem. The EGLP/TDPP investment configuration affords both a property owner in foreclosure and a qualified cash investor (PCI) a unique way for each to "safely invest" as limited partners together. It offers a positive solution that will rescue "all" of the property equity from a pending foreclosure for the owner to invest. The EGLP offers a fresh financial start for the owner by turning the currently financial insolvent owners into qualified investor. The investment capital gathered is invested for the benefit of the property owner rescued from foreclosure. The EGLP pays a profit share to the owner, and this grows the owner's rescued equity amount.

EGLP SPECIAL PERFORMANCE
The EGLP is particularly designed to:
- Introduce secured investment funds in a different and better way to cure a Notice of Default that the owner could not cure because; the property in foreclosure is leveraged at 65% or higher; the property owner is currently financially insolvent. Both the property itself and the owner do not qualify to borrow the money needed. However, the EGLP can provide the necessary funds to help the owner solve the problem.
- Rescues 100% of the property equity for the owner and makes it grow substantially, instead of the owner losing all the equity, because the owner could not cure the default in time.
- Change a potential sale under duress by the owner, which would amount to a give way for pennies on the dollar because it is in the process of being foreclosed upon, into a sale at "arms-length" that will achieve a full value sale for the owner.
- *Immediately* change a financially insolvent property owner into a qualified "cash" investor by having the owner use the rescued equity as investment capital so that the equity can substantially grow in amount.

- Grant the secured investor individual legal positions in the EGLP that provides extraordinary legal, financial, and reward protections never offered to an investor in a real estate transaction. This set of investor protections coupled with a "Bonus" payment plan adds up for the investor to a very safe and rewarding investment!
- Fashion original real estate transactions. The plan shapes and creates ways to operate "standard every day real estate transactions" that result in improved overall performance. In addition, there are original techniques designed, using the ability achieved with the large operational and investment fund, that fashion "unique brand-new real estate transactions". This large growing operating and investment fund can treat and solve investment problems as well as creating unique investment scenarios.

EGLP IS REALLY NEW
EGLP has:
- A self-generating system of raising investment capital
- A bona fide solution that rescues equity from loss due to foreclosure
- A secured cash investor position within a limited partnership
- A new type of property investor and qualified cash investor in a limited partnership
- A protection is made for and favors one secured investor (PCI)
- An avenue for owners to recover financially and financially grow
- A first-time investment risk-reward combination
- A first-time never-before created real estate transactions.

OWNERS FORECLOSURE POSITION
A typical property owner in foreclosure needs the EGLP/TDPP to cure the Notice of Default to help the owner. A property's debt structure is highly leveraged, and the owner is financially insolvent due to a pending foreclosure. Under these circumstances, it is very difficult to borrow more money to cure the foreclosure. This leaves the owner searching for a friend or relative to lend the money to save a substantial amount of equity left in the property. The owner's effort generally fails as their borrowing power is next to nil when in foreclosure. This situation occurs hundreds of thousands of times each year in the United States. History proves this beyond question!

If a property owner is unsuccessful in solving the foreclosure their retirement nest egg will be lost. The ability for the EGLP to rescue all the equity and invest it for the property owner is a method of advancement of considerable significance. The EGLP has been developed to especially rescue property equity from foreclosure to invest and grow the rescued amount. The achievement of structuring advanced legal, financial, and investment techniques in a demonstrable way makes the rescue possible. The owners need the TDPP in the EGLP to help solve the foreclosure's financial and legal problems to avoid losing the remaining equity. The lender is not a bad person, there is no other way to protect the money lent by the lender except through foreclosure. Foreclosure is the single and only solution the marketplace offers to protect the lender from a serious loss if the owner cannot cure the foreclosure.

THE OWNERS ARE REALLY HELPED
The TDPP allows the EGLP to financially and legally cure the owner's foreclosure in an original way. It also allows the EGLP to arrange for a currently insolvent property owner to continue investing as a qualified investor. The EGLP is a one-of-a-kind Limited Partnership with first-time answer for the serious foreclosure problem of the property owner and society. Using the property rescued equity as capital the owner becomes an investor partner in the EGLP with many other rescued property owners. Each owner earns a profit share as a partner that grows the equity rescued from each partner. An avenue for the

owner to recover financially and continue to grow financially is a unique answer found only in the EGLP/TDPP. A fair financial solution for the owner to avoid foreclosure is established for the ever first time ever.

The Equity Rescue Program rescues all the owner's equity, solves all negative legal and financial problems a foreclosure would cause, and affords the owner a new opportunity to earn a substantial income. This is instead of the owner being at the mercy of a foreclosure profit speculator or a forced sale at a foreclosure auction. When the property owner cannot cure the foreclosure Equity Rescue can. It is a superior and only way for a property owner in foreclosure, who cannot pay or attract the amount of default, to find the money needed to rescue all their property equity! The EGLP will rescue many property equities one at a time for owners. The EGLP grows the total amount of equities rescued by investing in real estate opportunities. The profit earned is shared with all limited partner property owners in the EGLP. A large segment of the property owners can now avoid losing the property equity to foreclosure.

Look what happens for the owner:
- The owner's foreclosure is cured,
- The owner accomplishes a full value sale,
- The owner has all the equity rescued,
- The owner becomes a limited partner investor with a substantial return on the equity,
- Avoids legal and financial serious negative consequences of a foreclosure,
- Gains valuable time to financially reorganize,
- Joins the Equity Rescue Trust Deed Pledge Plan for free.

THE PCI SECURED INVESTED CASH IN THE EGLP DOES A LOT
- Creates money to add to the EGLP asset total and lower the amount of investor risk.
- Creates money to immediately cure a property foreclosure.
- Creates money to establish an EGLP Financial Support Plan.
- Creates money that ensures partial loan(s) payments if necessary.
- Creates money to change a "duress sale" into an "arms-length transaction".
- Creates money to procure the first three EGLP foreclosure properties.
- Creates any fix-up or sale preparation cost.
- Creates financial encouragement for the EGP to join ER.
- Creates enough time for the EGLP to sell the property.

LOOK WHAT THE EGLP "PIVILEGE CASH INVESTOR" GAINS
The EGLP greatly improves foreclosure real estate investing. A qualified investor always wants and needs a safe and rewarding investment. The EGLP Identifies a new secured safe and highly rewarding investment in a very original way for a PCI. Investing is much safer because of several designed PCI protections and advantages granted in the EGLP.
In The EGLP:
- The PCI approves collateral.
- PCI dual collateral is made up of a real property ownership pledge and EGLP cash that increases with sales.
- PCI is favored with legal, timing, and reward advantages.
- The PCI funds invested are secured.
- A PCI has a secured investment with a substantial pre-agreed fixed bonus amount.
- A fixed bonus amount system to pay PCI.

- The EGLP has strong investment protections for the PCI with an attractive reward paid.
- The EGLP lowers the PCI risk in the EGLP by establishing a cash reserve plan.
- The EGLP grants the PCI a high return, and no management or legal responsibility.
- The investors have an acceleration plan opportunity that increases the rate of return.
- PCI is separate from the financially insolvent owners in all respects.
- Quick timing three EGLP sales and PCI is paid.
- Protects PCI using legal positions and keeps all decision making away from the owner.
- Avoids any possibility of a PCI bankruptcy or foreclosure involvement.
- Has EGLP investment acceleration opportunity.

EGLP HAS A NEW INVESTOR BONUS REWARD SYSTEM
- The bonus is a pre-agreed 42.5% of the amount of capital and it is a fixed amount that cannot go up or go down.
- The EGLP pays the PCI bonus. The EGLP agrees to reimburse the owner's capital account in the EGLP the funds used to pay the PCI bonus. The funds to reimburse the owners' capital accounts will come out of the gross profits earned from EGLP investments. In actuality, the bonus paid to the PCI is an EGLP expense and the PCI and EGP'S have an expense-free investment!
- A "Bonus Payment Plan" that pays a cash investor a pre-agreed bonus equal to 42.5% of the capital invested by the PCI is paid out of the net sales proceeds of the total of the first three EGLP properties sold. Forty-two and one-half percent (42.5%) of the $60,000 invested by the PCI equals a PCI Bonus of $25,500.
- The bonus is earned immediately when the PCI puts funds into escrow, and the bonus is paid to the PCI out of the third EGLP sale.
- The bonus is secured by a PTD that is recorded by the escrow against the property being used as the collateral for the PCI invested funds. The PCI approves collateral.
- The PCI is not dependent to be paid the bonus out of any EGLP profit venture results.
- The bonus timing is based on the time it takes to sell three EGLP properties.
- The bonus amount is generally a higher amount of profit than what a normal trust deed and other real estate investments yield.
- The EGLP acceleration plan increases the size, timing, and return rate of bonuses. The bonus growth can be accelerated by the PCI contracting with the General Partner in advance to turn over funds to invest in an agreed number of EGLP'S.

LOOK AT THE REAL ESTATE BROKER POSITION
- Real Estate Brokers can now associate with a plan that will have in time many properties for sale and each sale will raise substantial operating and investment capital. This combination of properties for sale and investment capital at the same time allows for unique transactions and investments to be conceived and implemented.
- The Equity Rescue Program offers the real estate broker original and valuable abilities.
- Brokers can now have a "safe" listing of property taken out of the foreclosure process to sell where it was once risky to handle.
- Brokers in new ways can earn new type of real estate finder fees and commissions.
- Brokers can now for the first time really help a property owner solve a serious foreclosure problem in a fair and just way by working with Equity Rescue.
- Brokers will have a non-bank source to fund financial problems on all types of properties.
- The plan can help any financially troubled property not just property in foreclosure.

- Brokers can now be associated with a plan that will have in time many different types and priced properties to list for sale. The combination of having several properties for sale and a large investment fund to work with, at the same time, will allow Brokers to complete real estate transactions in ways never contemplated.

THE EGLP HAS NEW TECHNIQUES

The EGLP/TDPP has first-time investment, legal, financial and operational techniques created. The plan is not similar in any way to the standard everyday foreclosure investment structure. There are several key elements of law used, and specially designed investment strategies introduced for the first time. The special combination of laws used together in the EGLP/TDPP that have never been designed as one group before. These individual parts working together in a limited partnership allow for new ability and an exceptionally good result.

THE EGLP HAS NEW FEATURES

Brand new are:
- Unique exclusive limited partnership design
- Unique legal, financial, and investment innovations
- Investment opportunity for financially insolvent owner
- A state-of-the-art secured foreclosure investment opportunity for a cash investor
- A new process for raising operating and investment capital
- Exclusive and innovative ways to earn income in real estate. The creativity in the EGLP/TDPP is innovative, original, and very valuable to its member partners.

NEW WAYS THE EGLP OPERATES

What is established for the first time in the EGLP/TDPP that is unique and valuable:
- New type cash investor is established
- New type property investor is established
- New way to qualify property owners to become investors is established
- A bonus type cash investor is established
- A way to secure an investor in a partnership is established
- Investor bonus payment system is established
- A way to earn personal income and profit is established
- A way to invest in foreclosure properties is established
- A new way to approach solving a foreclosure is established
- A way to attract investment capital is established
- A way to secure equity from foreclosure is established
- A new EGLP debt to asset ratio is established
- A way to invest property in foreclosure is established
- A way to invest cash in foreclosures is established
- A way to take a conditional title into an LP is established
- A way to favor one limited partner in an EGLP is established
- A new way to use a performance trust deed is established
- A new collateral system is established
- An Investment acceleration plan is established
- A dual class of limited partners is established.

NEW PROCEDURAL UNIQUENESS

The EGLP/TDPP has many individual salient workings that are a part of the whole plan that are very new. The EGLP creates and provides the following first-time ever procedural arrangements in a limited partnership.

They are:

- Using a legally established Deed of Trust Pledge (DTP) in a new way to bring partners with different roles together in a safe way to accomplish their needs and desires.
- Using a DTP to secure the collateral given to the PCI.
- Using a DTP to legally enforce the collection of PCI collateral.
- Advancing funds to cure a foreclosure for the owners, who could not pay the arrearage themselves, and when no lender would lend to the owners.
- Legally establishing a new type of dual collateral concept in a Limited partnership.
- Creating a "Priority Use Position" (PUP) on EGLP cash for one limited partner.
- Establishing a second way to be successful for the cash investor, in case of a default, creates a very low-risk factor for the investor.
- Establishing a legal right to property title, not just a portion of the equity, as collateral to secure the invested capital.
- Creating a legal pre-agreed fixed amount of bonus reward, and a new payment system for rewarding the PCI.
- Making a non-qualified insolvent investor (property owner in foreclosure) into a qualified investor in an EGLP.

WHAT THE EGLP DOES NOT DO

A little help can be given now by just letting it be known what is not happening in the Equity Rescue Plan. Equity Rescue is not doing the following things:

- Equity Sharing,
- Foreclosure speculating for profit,
- Short Sales,
- Flipping Property in anyway,
- Loan Modification.

Here are major operational differences from how standard foreclosure transaction works. The TDPP in the EGLP has unique procedural differences:

- NO purchase of the property ownership is made by the partnership.
- NO possession of the property by the EGLP takes place.
- NO profit is made on the property rescued by the partnership.
- NO money is given over to the owner from the partnership.
- NO promissory note is made or involved in the transaction.
- NO transfer of a "fee ownership interest" to the EGLP takes place.
- NO possession of the foreclosure property takes place by the EGLP.
- NO money for the EGLP is taken or received from the owner.
- NO EGLP expense is charged to the investor or the owner.
- NO investor cash reserves are necessary.
- NO EGLP foreclosure or bankruptcy is possible for the PCI to be involved in ever.

NO LOAN REQUIRED
- The EGLP receives the necessary operating capital from the PCI investment.
- There is no additional investment money needed to complete the TDPP in the EGLP.
- The EGLP has no need or reason to apply for a loan to start operating the EGLP.
- There is no loan in the EGLP TDPP created by or for anyone, no loan law apples! No loan is taken "subject to" or "assumed" in the TDPP, so the federal act does not apply.
- The owner remains legally responsible for the property loan. No property sale, ownership interest, or loan transfer is made by the owner to the EGLP.

WHAT DOESN'T HAPPEN
- The EGLP never owns the beneficial right to the owner's property equity.
- None of the money invested by the PCI is ever given by the EGLP to the property owner.
- The owner in foreclosure never pays a dime for the service provided.
- The PCI is paid from property sales but replaced by the gross income of the EGLP!
- When the property is sold at a full market value price, the EGLP does not receive a dime of the net sales proceeds for itself.

LOOK WHAT IS DONE IN THE EGLP
Here are items of the EGLP/TDPP that are brand new:
- General Partner takes only Bare Title to the property.
- Rescues equity from being lost because of a foreclosure in a new way.
- Creates a secured transaction in a limited partnership for one cash investor.
- Introduces "secured investor" funds that are used to cure the foreclosure and rescue equity.
- Arranges a different risk-reward scenario for partners in the partnership.
- Makes investing very safe and rewarding with new legal and investment techniques.
- Arranges millions of investment dollars to invest.
- Favors one Partner's legal and investment position.
- Arranges two separate contractual positions for the PCI.
- Arranges a pledge of a "foreclosure free" fee ownership of a property as collateral.
- Grants an EGLP Performance Trust Deed (PTD) in favor of the PCI and records it against the collateral property chosen by the PCI.
- Changes a financially insolvent property owner into a "cash investor" by having the owner use the rescued equity as investment capital in the EGLP.
- Invests and grows the rescued equity for the owner's benefit.
- Cures the foreclosure on the property chosen by the PCI, the property is no longer in foreclosure.
- Changes the value of the property, it becomes market value as the property is no longer in foreclosure and subject to low offers.
- Changes a sale under duress of foreclosure that would be a give-a-way for pennies on the dollar into a "marketplace full value sale" for the owner.
- Establishes an EGLP financial support plan to insures property loan payments will be made, if necessary.
- Supplies the collateral security in place before the PCI places money into the escrow!
- Generates and grows a partnership "Operating and Investment Fund" accomplished by rescuing property equities from foreclosure and turning the equities into the owner's investment capital in the EGLP.
- Arranges new money in the EGLP and uses the TDPP for solutions to various financially troubled properties and new investments.

- Originates first-time investment transactions and improves standard transactions with substantial capital available to make it possible.
- Creates a new way to use a Performance Trust Deed to secure a pledge of property ownership.
- Creates the ability to interact EGLPs as tenant-in-common, solve financially troubled property problems, and handle high-value property in foreclosure.

EGLP's NEW "LEGAL" USE COMPOSITE
- Using a Partnership as a Three-Party Contract
- Using a Partnership for Dual Purposes
- Using a PTD To Secure a Pledge
- Using a Capital Gains Tax Deferral Plan
- Using a No Cost Bare Title Concept
- Using a Property Equities to Pay Bonus
- Using Many LPs to Favor Just One LP.
- Using EGLP Cash That Has Spending Restriction
- Using Sales Proceeds as Start-up Capital

EGLP RELEVANT CATOGORIES
The EGLP is truly a newly designed partnership that operates in a new advanced way for the good of its partners. The EGLP has many new operating techniques. By category here is a list of important ones.

LIMITED PARTNERS:
The PCI investment position in a limited partnership has never been designed before now. New first-time legal positions that protect the PCI are:
- Creates two classes of partners with separate roles for each individual protection.
- Deed of Trust Pledge position.
- Priority Use Position.
- Grant Deed right position.
- Unique collateral collection position.
- Financial Support plan.
- New legal & safe way to advance funds to cure a foreclosure.
- Secured transactions within a limited partnership.
- An extremely large investment fund is created in each EGLP. In addition, the PCI does not have any legal liability for EGLP operations and enjoys a high reward in quick time with no managerial involvement to agree to invest.

EGLP INVESTMENT:
Special EGLP investment characteristics:
- Fixed bonus amount
- Growing rescued equity
- Dual collateral position
- PCI has two ways to succeed
- Timing is shorter on average
- Expanded legal positions
- Low personal time and risk
- No owner loan payment problem
- PCI quick collateral collection system

- Property is maintained by a partner
- PCI has no foreclosure or bankruptcy concern.

COLLATERAL
Special EGLP events:
- Property fee title Is the collateral.
- Arranged raising operating and investment capital in a profoundly new way.
- Introduced an equity-rich property as collateral to secure the PCI funds.
- Provides two types of collateral for the same investor funds that protect the PCI.
- Minimizes the risk factor for the investor by introducing cash as collateral.
- Creates a unique Financial Support Plan to maintain the collateral amount.
- Increases PCI collateral with each property sale.
- This newly designed collateral arrangement makes the decision to invest in the EGLP a safe and confident one for the PCI.

FINANCIAL
In the EGLP is:
- Created an original way to solve many types of real estate financing problems.
- Created two classes of partners with separate capital accounts.
- Figured out how to increase the collateral security for the PCI as EGLP sales are made.
- Created a unique financial support plan within an EGLP.
- Created an original way to solve many types of real estate financing problems.
- Using PCI capital for both operating and investment purposes.
- Paying bonus with a pre-agreed fixed bonus amount to an investor instead of a profit share.

LEGAL
The EGLP:
- Grants several legal positions to protect the PCI.
- Creates secured Transaction in a L.P.
- Uses a Performance Deed of Trust Pledge to secure a pledge.
- Pays the investor a fixed-amount bonus.
- Grants the investor the right to determine what his/her capital is spent on.
Uses investor funds for operating and investments.

A NEW WAY OF RAISING INVESTMENT & OPERATING CAPITAL
A new groundbreaking method and ability to raise large sums of investment capital has been created. The fund is called the Operating and Investment Fund (O&IF) in the EGLP. Because there has been an original transaction designed, that can rescue property equity from being foreclosure upon, a new method for gathering large sums of operating and investment capital on a repeat never-ending basis has been developed.

The "Trust Deed Pledge Plan" (TDPP) in the Equity Growth Limited Partnership (EGLP) rescues the full amount of equity in the property using the TDPP. The plan allows the owner in foreclosure to cure the foreclosure and achieve market value. The owner becomes an investor to grow the equity rescued which will create future purchasing power.

This has never been accomplished before; it features a one-of-a-kind exclusive ability! Raising large sums of capital to invest is how the Equity Rescue Program can help solve many different types of property money problems. By raising large sums of capital repeatedly, $72,000 to over $100,000 property net equity rescued on average time after time, using the TDPP, many financial property problems that were not able to be approached financially before can now be solved. This is because enough money necessary will be available to address difficult property money problems safely and profitably.

The first Equity Rescue idea discovered was "how" to rescue property equity from foreclosure" for the benefit of the property owner. As a result, an idea of equal importance to rescuing property equity was also discovered. A far advanced way of gathering a never-ending always-growing partnership operating and investment capital was created.

Rescuing the property equity for the owners and "turning the owners into investors" using their rescued equities creates the O&IF. An O&IF will be established in each of several EGLPs. A system of generating and consolidating operating large sums of capital is used by the EGLP to operate and invest.

Solving a property owner's most serious financial problem they most likely will ever encounter in their life is very gratifying. However, it is not the purpose that the Equity Rescue Program was developed. The main reason was and is to earn income by creating an O&IF, that will raise large sums of operating and investment capital in a partnership, for the purpose of investing in and solving all types of financially troubled real estate properties. The Equity Rescue Program is not just for solving foreclosure properties, with the O&IF it does much more.

WHO NEEDS THE O&IF CAPITAL, EVERYONE DOES!
The EGLP capital raised provides an answer for a large part of the problematic financial section of the real estate market. Financially troubled properties in foreclosure and non-foreclosure financially troubled properties can be solved using the O&IF in EGLP/TDPP. The TDPP can arrange financial answers that other investors would or could not do.

RISK IS VERY IMPORTANT
The risk for one person or entity in many financially troubled property situations is high and deters investors from attempting the investment. The EGLP lowers the risk because of the ability it must provide as much capital as is needed to ensure success. From several EGLPs to be formed in the future, that will invest together, a new financial ability is created.

A SPECIAL POINT HERE
Many financial problems on properties are dismissed as unsolvable because of the amount of the money necessary to solve the problem. The EGLP cooperation with each other provides a large amount of capital to solve many different types of real estate money problems. As the amount of capital needed becomes available the most difficult property financial problem can be solved.

Several EGLPs, each with its own growing O&IF, can financially interact to solve difficult real estate problems. The same GP allows for the EGLPs to invest as "Tenant in Common". This EGLP ability to interact with each other provides substantial backup funding to make the profitable investment strong and safe.

OPERATING AND INVESTMENT CAPITAL POTENTIAL
As a result of helping property owners avoid foreclosure and rescue their equity to become investors, the ability to build an "ever-increasing never-ending" O&IF is created. Never has such a legal and financial method been developed that has the capability to gather so much investment capital into a limited partnership to invest for profit.

So, now with the legal key that opens this operating and investing funding door, we can look at what can be developed in the realm of real estate investing. The first question is how much capital can be raised? The amount of each O&IF will grow exponentially and perform in many original and prolific ways. The accumulated amount will allow for extremely safe and rewarding investments to be formulated for the first time. With a steady stream of operating capital to work with, first-time financial solutions are now possible.

Equity Rescue's O&IF will constantly grow because, daily, thousands of foreclosures are occurring throughout the United States. Foreclosure is simply a Lender's collateral collection process, it is a mechanism that is built to protect the lender, and it will always continue forever. Many properties continually going into foreclosure will simply grow the O&IF exponentially. The financial power of such a large capital investment fund will be enormous. The O&IF expands the depth and scope of Equity Rescue's financial investment power.

Understanding how the fund will grow is to realize the investment financial power it delivers. The O&IF makes it possible with this much investment capital to construct new investment techniques and transactions. All types of property financial problems can be entertained with real solutions that will work and produce a profit. The fund provides unique investment ability because of a process that allows for financially safe and lucrative investment in several categories. Adjusting standard structural investment designs used today, to improve performance and results, is possible with this constantly growing amount of capital.

With the O&IF all kinds of real estate opportunities can be entertained to invest in for profit. The EGLP will have the ability to perform new transactions that were previously not possible, and it will have a considerable amount of backup funds to ensure financial success. This means EGLP investments will be financially strong, safe, and rewarding.

The Equity Rescue Program's Market is not limited to just the foreclosure market. Or just to residential properties. Equity Rescue's ability to raise large amounts of operating and investment capital for the EGLP to invest in makes it possible to deal with a wide range of different types of properties.

EGLP INVESTMENT CAPITAL SOURCES

You will see as we go along that in addition to the O&IF garnering investment capital to operate with, in the EGLP, there are more ways that raise additional investment capital because of and in addition to the O&IF achieved. A large amount of capital accumulation, from several other sources, in addition to the O&IF achievement, is important and a special message to understand! Here is the question? What would you do if you had access to large sums of capital to invest in real estate that continues to grow in amount?

There is Joint Venturing with the EGLP. The EGLP can offer an investor partner (with capital to invest) an opportunity to share profits 50-50 and have two additional advantages the EGLP will provide. There will be an agreement if additional cash is needed because of an initial cost estimate overrun, the EGLP will provide it without charge to the profit picture. The financial money will be provided by the EGLP O&IF with a favorable rate of interest. In time the property owner rescued can sell the limited partner share to the EGLP at a discount rate. 50-50 is a common thought. This would be the choice of the owner after the EGLP is operating at a healthy financial clip. Or the EGP can change into a PCI position by starting a new EGLP. MORE CAPITAL TO USE WITH JV PARTNER INVESTING.

EGLP PROFIT CREATED AND USED UNTIL END OF EGLP
Profit earned is profit used to invest until the EGLP dissolves. MORE CAPITAL TO REINVEST COMES IN FROM EGLP INVESTMENTS CONCLUDED!

"ADDITIONAL" CAPITAL COMES FROM THE PCI REINVESTMENT
Now looking at the PCI investment in an EGLP one might conclude that this is an exceptionally fine investment. One in which an investor would like to repeat as many times as possible. So, look here for more capital coming into the EGLP as fast as the market will allow. MORE CAPITAL TO USE TO INVEST!

ANSWER FOR ALL TYPES OF FINANCIALLY TROUBLED PROPERTIES
- Foreclosure Properties
- Negative Cash Flow Portfolios
- Earthquake Retrofit Properties
- Investment Portfolio Properties
- Tax Problem Properties
- Fixer-Upper Properties
- Brownfield Properties
- Tear down the old structure and build a new structure

EQUITY RESCUE MARKET IS AN OPEN MARKET WITH NO LIMITATION
The Equity Rescue Program's Market is not limited to just the foreclosure market. Or just to residential properties. Equity Rescue's ability to raise large amounts of operating and investment capital for the EGLP to invest, its main purpose, makes it possible to deal with a wide range of properties. The numbers are staggering. A Fair estimate of all types, residential, commercial, retail, apartments, land, etc. of properties on which a Notice of Default has been filed is approximately one million (1,000,000) each year in the United States. This represents billions of dollars of lost property equity by the owners and businesses each year because of foreclosure!

It only takes a few of the properties to qualify for the Equity Rescue Program when compared to the number of properties that have a pending foreclosure. The TDPP in the EGLP can raise millions of dollars rescuing property rescue and reinvesting it to earn profit for all involved. There are more than enough properties each year to build the most proficient system to raise investment capital in America and Canada.

EQUITY RESCUE IS A NATIONWIDE PROGRAM! It is not necessary for an investor to be in any state to enjoy the benefits of being a PCI. Loans and other financial problems and investment projects are incurring in every state and will need funds from the EGLP O&IF to finance them. Do not limit your thinking. Think about all the many possibilities for earning from properties all over the United States!

The average value of residential property in the United States currently is approximately $300,000 and will yield approximately $72,000 net equity when sold by the EGLP. History indicates the number of ongoing in-process default notices in the United States will be approximately one million (1,000,000) or more each year. For 5 years the total equals five million (5,000,000) Notices of Defaults in progress in the United State. If one percent (1%) qualified each year it would be 10,000 properties qualifying. Over five years the total number would be 50,000.

Multiplying $72,000 average net equity left in the 50,000 qualifying properties and the capital potential would be THREE BILLION SIX HUNDRED MILLION $3,600,000,000 DOLLARS in potential investment capital. What if the percentage is higher over five years? What if the percentage qualifying for Equity Rescue is three percent (3%), four percent (4%), or even five percent (5%)? For one to think that any one of these percentages is the number qualifying each year is not outlandish.

The following information was taken from the internet, it has not been confirmed by the author. September 2021 foreclosures are up from last month, as well as compared to last year. Here are 2021 rates of foreclosure filings per housing unit for large population states. You can see there are a very large number of foreclosures in just these five states.

NOTE: go to the internet at any time and get up-to-date monthly reports. No matter what date it happens to be, there will always be more than enough property owners needing the EGLP TDPP to help them from losing their property equity!

FLORIDA
Florida nabbed the number one spot for the highest foreclosure rate in September with one in every 3,276 homes going into foreclosure. The third most populated state in the country has a total of 9,448,159 housing units of which 2,884 went into foreclosure. The counties with the most foreclosures per housing unit were (from highest to lowest): Bradford, Broward, Pasco, Miami-Dade, and Union.

ILLINOIS
Illinois managed to slide out of the top spot for highest foreclosure rate, taking the number two spot in September. Of its 5,360,315 homes, 1,528 went into foreclosure, making the sixth most populated state's foreclosure rate one in every 3,508. The counties with the most foreclosures per housing unit were (from highest to lowest): Peoria, Will, Clay, Clark, and Madison.

CALIFORNIA
The most populated state ranked ninth in September for most foreclosures. Of its 14,175,976 housing units, 2,763 went into foreclosure, making California's foreclosure rate one in every 5,131 households. The counties with the most foreclosures per housing unit were (from highest to lowest): Merced, San Bernardino, Kern, San Joaquin, and El Dorado.

TEXAS
The Lone Star State saw 1,179 foreclosures in September. With a foreclosure rate of one in every 9,277 households, this put the second most populous state with 10,937,026 housing units into the 22nd spot. The counties with the most foreclosures per housing unit were (from highest to lowest): Wilbarger, Liberty, Carson, Brown, and Scurry.

NEW YORK
With 752 out of a total of 8,322,722 housing units going into foreclosure in September, the fourth most populated state took the 27th spot with a foreclosure rate of one in every 11,067 households. The counties with the most foreclosures per housing unit were (from highest to lowest): Montgomery, Suffolk, Otsego, Sullivan, and Orleans.

You can imagine as I have those the other 45 states, although each is smaller than any one of these five, the combined total of all the 45 is most likely is more than the total of the five states. I think this is a reasonable assumption even though assuming can be dangerous. The point is the total number of foreclosures filed each year in all fifty states is very large indeed!

AVERAGE $300,000 PROPERTY RESCUE ESTIMATE
$300,000 + Appraised value
$180,000 - 60% LTV
$ 15,000 - NOD Late Payments 5% LTV

$105,000 + Gross Property Equity
$ 21,000 - 7% Selling Commission
$ 12,000 - Closing Cost
$ 72,000 + Net Equity to Rescue and Invest in the EGLP

A MILLION-DOLLAR PROPERTY NOTICE OF DEFAULT ESTIMATE

There is a saying, "the bigger they are the harder they fall". Many high-priced properties receive a Notice of Default is recorded against them each year! How many million-dollar properties are they like this? The answer is an awful lot!

$1,000,000 + Appraised Property Value
$ 600,000 - 60% Loan Principal Balance
$ 50,000 - 05% NOD Late Payments & Foreclosure Costs
$ 350,000 + Gross Property Equity
$ 70,000 - 07% Sale Commission
$ 30,000 - Transferring Title to EGLP & Selling Closing Cost
_____
$ 250,000 + Owner Net Equity to Rescue and Invest in the EGLP

NOTE

Depending on the amount and the owner's need the equity amount that will be invested can be negotiated. It is not necessary for the owner in some cases to invest the whole amount of equity rescue. The reason will prevail, helping the owner is the goal!

Understand the owner is in real financial difficulty. The bigger they are the harder they fall. However, with a million-dollar property and $250,000 in net equity the owner could 1) negotiate with a profit speculator so the owner could retain say half of the equity. Not a total loss, 2) BUT IF THEY JOIN, THEY SAVE IT ALL. How, if an owner will take half for him/herself, Equity Rescue can agree to split the sale proceed in half also. One-half cash out of escrow for the owner and one-half INVESTED IN THE EGLP! Different situations require different answers.

An original foreclosure answer that property owners badly need, is created. The foundation of this fresh approach features a new attitude towards the property owner in foreclosure. The owner under severe financial duress is helped to become a qualified investor in a new exclusive arrangement. The entire equity in the property is rescued and grows with profit share while all the present and future ugly consequences of a foreclosure are avoided for the owners. This answer is not found in any other investment and is truly a unique development that saves a financial catastrophe from occurring to the owner.

THE EGLP CAN DO WHAT OTHER PARTNERSHIPS CANNOT

It organizes a way to start the TDPP in the EGLP wherein the secured PCI is greatly favored in a new structure. It gathers a unique set of legal, financial, and investment investor positions that greatly favor the PCI. EGLP capital is raised by establishing a low-risk high-return secured system of investment for a PCI. This new scenario is legally and financially very favorable to a PCI. To the point that it attracts an infusion of PCI operating cash into the EGLP. Original innovative real estate investments transactions of all kinds take place because of the TDPP financial structure.

The EGLP can advance funds to cure an owner's property foreclosure when no one else would. It provides a better safer way to invest in all types of real estate, not just foreclosures. It can solve many difficult real estate financial problems for the first time. Real estate brokers, investors, lenders, and property owners substantially gain financially from the EGLP's ability to create safe more rewarding investments. All financially troubled properties are possible to help and improve to earn a profit using the EGLP. The EGLP/TDPP is a major accomplishment in many ways.

An original investor investment model is created. The Plan is carefully designed to avoid any investor loss from happening. The investor's capital is secured from the point of commitment to completion and there is no management or legal responsibility for the investor in the Plan. The investor is granted new and separate legal positions with major financial advantages that form a first-time investment innovation!

The EGLP/TDPP changes investing in foreclosure into an exceptionally safe and highly rewarding investment structure and procedure for a cash investor. The TDPP Privilege Cash Investor (PCI) has strong built-in legal and investment protections. Substantial collateral, a new financial arrangement, and a different legal combination together establish a strong and rewarding investment. The PCI is handsomely compensated for providing the EGLP start-up money on a secured basis. The PCI secured scenario stands out because it is very safe, rewarding, and timely. The way the TDPP brings the owner and a secured cash investor together in the EGLP greatly benefits both.

New is a different way to pay the secured cash investor. A pre-agreed fixed amount as the investor reward is pre-agreed to up front and is paid in approximately one year. The reward is a minimum of $25,500 to a maximum of $42,500 for the investor. A small investment amount by each member in a group or a minimum of $60,000 up to $100,000 in a single amount can be invested. Within the TDPP a new investment technology enters the market designed to ensure the return of the PCI investment capital along with the financial reward promised.

LENDING INDUSTRY GAINS
The lenders gain from a financial standpoint, which has a very positive and substantial effect on their business. Currently, lenders are required by the federal government to set aside a large reserve for each loan in default. The reserves are sitting idle and not earning taxable revenue. The reserve requirement is eating away at their profit margins. Lenders will appreciate the financial improvement by having bad loans cured and taken off the books. The lenders also with the reduction in federal government reserves will have more money to lend.

THE EGLP ACTIVITY ACCELERATES
The PCI reinvestment plan will increase the rate of return on invested capital while lowering the risk of each PCI investment in an EGLP. As each property is taken out of foreclosure and sold acceleration occurs in the EGLP:
- The PCI bonus accelerates and grows with reinvestment.
- The O&IF accelerates.
- The number of owner properties in an EGLP accelerates.
- The number of EGLPs that can be opened accelerates.
- The amount of capital raised in the EGLP accelerates.
- The number of investments using the capital raised accelerates.

THE EGLP CRITICAL CASH CAPITAL "FINANCIAL SUPPORT PLAN"
The PCI $60,000 investment in the EGLP is called "Critical Cash Capital" (CCC). This money creates a "Financial Support Plan" which starts the EGLP operating and fulfills the initial EGLP cash requirement.

THE $60,000 INVESTED BY THE PCI IS USED TO:
- Start up the EGLP.
- Cure the property foreclosure and prepare it for sale.
- Financially support the property until a sale occurs, if necessary.
- Provide $10,000 of the $60,000 CCC for EGLP expenses.

THE ADVANTAGES CREATED BY ADDING CASH:
The PCI $60,000 Creates:
- Money that constructs an acceptable risk in the EGLP for the PCI.
- Money to cure the pending Foreclosure.
- Money to establish an EGLP Financial Support Plan.
- Money independence for EGLP by eliminating the need to borrow.
- Money that pays property payments of the owners, if necessary.
- Money changes negotiation under duress to arm's length negotiation.
- Money to cure and take into the EGLP three properties in foreclosure.
- Money to fix up and prepare the property for sale, if necessary.
- Money that encourages the EGP and PCI to join the EGLP.
- Money that will allow enough time for the EGLP to sell the property.
- Money as a reserve for the EGLP in case of unexpected problems.
- Money helps the EGLP to become financially self-sustaining in time.

The PCI will not invest money if the investment is not safe. If the PCI does not invest money, there is no way left to inject money. The PCI improves the DAR by creating a very safe investment by providing the cash to the EGLP.

EGLP MONEY INCOME

1ST MONEY SOURCE
The liquidity created by the PCI cash invested plus the owners making the monthly payment, to the degree they can, are key ingredients for the financial maintenance of the property rescued from foreclosure. The cash invested by the PCI is used to support the loan monthly payments for the mortgage on the property, if necessary. The PCI cash protects the property acting as collateral from going back into foreclosure and maintains the full value of the property. The added PCI cash is of sufficient size to support the property financially until it is sold for the owner's benefit.
- The money invested by the PCI starts the EGLP operating.
- The PCI money creates the unique EGLP Debt to Asset Ratio
- The PCI funds pay late payments to cure the Notice of Default.
- The PCI fund pays escrow costs to transfer the property.
- The PCI fund supports the loan payments until the property sells, if necessary.
- The PCI fund acts as an operating fund only for the EGLP, it cannot be invested.
- The PCI does a lot for the EGLP to earn the bonus by investing the funds.

The PCI $60,000 Creates Money:
- To cure the pending Foreclosure.
- To take into the EGLP three properties in foreclosure.
- To fix up and prepare the property for sale, if necessary.
- To establish an EGLP Financial Support Plan.
- The money constructs an acceptable risk in the EGLP for the PCI.

- The money pays property payments of the owners, if necessary.
- It encourages the PCI to safely join the EGLP.
- The PCI funds will allow enough time for the EGLP to sell the property.
- The PCI money takes the property out of foreclosure and changes negotiation under duress to an arm's length negotiation.
- The money creates independence for EGLP by eliminating the need to borrow.

2nd MONEY SOURCE

When each owner's property sells the owner, using the property's net sales proceeds of the property, becomes a cash investor in the EGLP. When the property owner becomes an investor, the net sales proceeds from the property sold become operating money for the EGLP. Twenty-five EGLP properties sold will generate approximately $2,000,000 or more in each EGLP capital account. As a result, the EGLP will have substantial investment funds to invest.

3rd MONEY SOURCE

Gross profit from EGLP investments is the third source of operating funds until the EGLP dissolves. The gross Profit of the EGLP pays operating expenses and the EGLP Net Profit is shared with the EGP partners.

WHAT HAPPENS TO THE EGLP MONEY

What happens to the money in the EGLP is different. The EGLP does not purchase the property in foreclosure but has control of selling the property. The EGLP never owns the beneficial right to the owner's property equity. In short, and making the point very clear, the EGLP does not make or ever take any money from the owner in foreclosure for the service it provides the owner. Not a dime!

The following list shows the PCI that the money issues are carefully thought out, to protect and favor the PCI:
- Two legal positions the PTD and AOP protect the PCI money.
- Automatic collection is achieved from the EGLP with the AOP and PTD.
- Legal structure is the investor's money enforcer.
- None of the money invested by the PCI is ever given by the EGLP to the property owner.
- The owner in foreclosure never pays a dime and the EGLP pays the PCI bonus from the gross income of the EGLP!
- When the property is sold at a full market value price, the EGLP does not receive a dime of the proceeds for itself.

Expenses paid from the PCI funds:
- Pays loan arrearage
- Fixes up for sale the preparation and pays escrow cost.
- Escrow transfer of title cost to EGLP
- Money paid for the monthly loan payment
- Expenses paid from the PCI fund invested are reimbursed out of the sale proceeds of the property and the fund is replenished after each EGLP property sale.
- Fund is used to procuring the first three EGLP properties.
- Arranges enough time for the EGLP to sell the property.
- Insures each property is acceptable legally, financially, and physically with an Appraisal report – Contractor Report – Preliminary Title Report.

DOUBLE PROTECTION

The TDPP combines the cash and a property title into a collateral package that secures the cash investor's capital in the EGLP. This new asset combination of cash and equity makes investing in the TDPP safe and practical. The PCI cash protects the property acting as collateral from going back into foreclosure by using the PCI invested to pay the mortgage payments which maintains and solidifies the full value of the property until it sells. The cash can be and is used to support the money requirements of the mortgage on the property, if necessary. The added PCI cash is of sufficient size required to sell the property for full price for the owner's benefit.

PAYOUTS

$ 9,000 PCI Finder Fee (Initially paid out of property equities)

$25,500 PCI Bonus (Initially paid out of property equities)

The PCI does not rely on the EGLP making a profit to pay the Finder Fee or the Bonus. The Bonus is paid out of three property sales and reimbursed out of EGLP profit earned. EGLP operating expenses are paid out of EGLP gross profit earned.

PCI CASH IS PUT INTO RESERVE

The cash in the EGLP is also used to create a Priority Use Position (PUP). A PUP is created in the Articles of The Partnership. The PUP establishes that all the partnership cash on hand from *partnership property sales* must be used by the partnership, before any of the PCI funds invested in the EGLP is used to take in more properties.

EGLP DEBT TO RATIO

The Debt to Asset Ratio (DAR) is changed by the cash amount invested from the PCI, the cash changes and improves the DAR. The Equity Rescue DAR creates a financial position that lowers and makes the investment risk factor acceptable. The percent of security goes up and the risk percentage goes down for the PCI in the TDPP. The PCI can invest safely and the EGLP can operate safely with the increase in cash.

MONEY CONSIDERATIONS

In addition to the safety created in the EGLP for the PCI by the many special legal positions, the EGLP has created a new limited partnership "Financial Support Plan" to financially service all the loans on the property contributed to the EGLP until the property is sold.

The purpose of the EGLP is to create the highest degree of security for the PCI'S invested fund possible that is called the Critical Cash Capital (CCC) in the EGLP Financial Support Plan. The PCI is investing in the EGLP at a critical moment in time in the EGLP so that it can start operations. The first item for the EGLP is to take the property out of the foreclosure process using the CCC funds to pay the Notice of Default to cure the foreclosure.

In addition to the cash reserve built into the financial support plan and the property equity, both acting as collateral, there is also income for the property owner paying the monthly loan payments until it sells. There is enough reserve cash projected in the amount of the financial support plan to financially support the property for the required time it takes to achieve a full price sale of the property.

The funds invested by the PCI, in addition to supplying the cash to cure the foreclosure, also acts as a reserve fund to pay the loan payments on the property if the loan for the property is not paid on time. There is enough reserve cash projected in the amount of the financial support plan to financially support the property for the required time it takes to achieve a full-price sale of the property. The EGP (former owner) is still responsible for paying the loan until it is sold.

If the owner cannot afford the full payment, then the EGLP will assist in paying the monthly payment on the property using its cash reserve fund. The reimbursement for such cash advancement comes out of the gross sales proceeds of the foreclosure property the owner contributed to the EGLP.

- The PCI investment money is the seed money to start the EGLP operating.
- The Financial Support Plan structured prevents a foreclosure from re-occurring.
- The owner will make the payments or the EGLP financial fund will, only if necessary.
- No reliance is made on the owner to keep the property out of foreclosure.
- There are two sources of funds to pay loan payments after curing the Notice of Default.

UNPARALLELED EGLP ACHIEVEMENTS

An original investment achievement. In addition to the secured Performance Trust Deed Investment for the cash investor there is other major investing improvements in the program.
Here are some examples:

- Portfolio Property Plan (A New Achievement)
  Creates an ability to restructure a portfolio by extracting the negative cash flowing properties while keeping them productive for the owner/investor.
- Joint Venture Plans (Amount of EGLP Capital Improves Safety)
  A special plan that offers a matching dollar-for-dollar investment funds plus low-cost financing with substantial cash reserves. No bank necessary!
- 1031 Exchange (Improves Ability with Cash Out Property Available in Advance) Several cash-out properties will become available over time as million-dollar properties go into foreclosure and must be sold by the EGLP.
- Tenant-In-Common (Total Buying and Selling with EGLPs Cooperating Together) A special ability divides and lowers the risk when dealing with high-value properties. The same General Partner for all the EGLP'S makes this possible.

PROCESS TO JOIN THE EGLP
PHASE 1

A Preliminary Understanding is given to each of the owners and the cash investor. After each has read how the EGLP TDPP works and agrees to the process the parties sign to show that they have read and understood their roles in the plan. The Preliminary Understanding is not a legally binding contract.

Then a qualifying property is located and accepted by the GP to offer to the PCI to approve as collateral to secure the PCI funds in the EGLP. The PCI receives three professional reports. An Appraisal, Contractor, and Preliminary Title Report is reviewed by the cash investor to verify the overall value and legal status of the foreclosure property. A PCI physical inspection of the property will be available prior to the PCI approving the property as collateral. After the PCI approval, all the parties then enter into a legal agreement the EGLP Articles of Partnership that recites all the terms, conditions, and procedures of the EGLP agreed to by the parties.

The owner's purpose in transferring the Bare Title to the property to the EGLP is to have the property fee ownership pledged as collateral to attract investment capital into the EGLP. The foreclosure is cured before the property is pledged as collateral. Upon the Grant Deed Bare Title transfer to the EGLP the owner is fulfilling a condition laid down in the Articles of Partnership.

The General Partner of the EGLP opens an escrow. To start the EGLP the escrow company is given the escrow instructions and proof establishing the legal status of the EGLP. The EGLP Articles of Partnership are presented for signature at the title company and upon signing by all the parties the EGLP operation begins. The PCI, owner, and GP are now legal partners after agreeing to the terms and conditions in the Articles of Partnership. The property owner deposits the Grant Deed that is transferring the Bare Title to the EGLP into the escrow as stipulated and agreed to in the Articles of Partnership by the owner and GP. This act creates the EGLP as the "holder" of the title of ownership according to the Articles of Partnership.

The EGLP accepts receipt out of escrow of a Grant Deed transferring the Bare Title. The Articles spell out the division of ownership of the grantor and grantee. The owner after transferring the Bare title retains possession and all equitable rights including responsibilities of ownership until the property is sold. The owner (Bare Title Grantor) retains the legal responsibility for the loan note signed by the owner. The EGLP has the legal right established in the Articles of Partnership to sell the property. The escrow records the transfer of the Grant Deed.

The owner's purpose in transferring Bare Title to the EGLP is to have the property foreclosure cured and to be able to offer a fee ownership pledge as collateral to attract investment capital into the EGLP. And to be able to sell the property for full value. Upon the Grant Deed Bare Title transfer to the EGLP the owner is fulfilling a condition laid down in the Articles.

The PCI deposits into escrow the funds agreed to that are necessary to begin operating the EGLP. The escrow company only after receiving the Grant Deed to the property from the owner receives the PCI investment funds. The escrow cures the foreclosure using the PCI cash invested.

The escrow company to take the property out of foreclosure uses the investment funds deposited by the PCI. The EGLP gives into escrow a Performance Trust Deed (PTD) in favor of the PCI, and it is recorded against the property in the land recorder's office. This occurs after the property is taken out of foreclosure. The PTD secures the collateral for the PCI funds invested.

The EGLP lists the property for sale with a Real Estate Broker. The EGLP with the PCI funds make sure that the loan payments are made, if necessary, under an agreement made with the owner in the Articles until the property is sold.

The EGLP sells the owner's property and transfers by Grant Deed Fee Simple Ownership to the property to the new owner. The property is sold, and the equity is rescued. The owner's condition in the Articles of Partnership Agreement to sell the property has been satisfied. The agreement between the EGLP and PCI is completed when the EGLP sells the third property, and the PCI leaves the EGLP.

The remaining property sales proceeds from the first three sales (now the EGLP operating and investment capital) are used to cure more foreclosure properties and rescue more equities. This is what builds the O&IF in each of several EGLPs that will be operating under the same General Partner. The EGLP invests the investment capital to earn a profit when the O&IF reaches an acceptable level.

EGLP PHASE 2
THE EGLP OPERATING AND INVESTMENT FUND BUILD-UP
Each property has the default notice cured by the escrow using the PCI investment funds. When a property is sold and closed then the equity has been rescued. This is repeated three times on three properties. The three properties are sold one at a time using brokers to sell the properties to new buyers.

The PCI funds invested are used to take in and sell the properties. After each sale, the PCI fund is replenished out of the sale money. The PCI is paid a Bonus and leaves the EGLP after three sales.

Additional owners join the EGLP to rescue their equity the same way as the first three properties. Only now the EGLP has operating money from prior property sales to use to cure the foreclosures without needing investor funds. NOTE: One owner may have more than one property in foreclosure! It could be that 25 owners with 35 properties join the EGLP.

Taking in owner properties and selling them this way establishes an Operating and Investment Fund that continues to grow in the EGLP. The build-up of the investment fund to approximately $2,000,000 or more per EGLP There will be several EGLPS in the United States and each will build a large operating and investment fund.

EGLP PHASE 3
INVESTING FOR PROFIT BEGINS
EGLP earns by investing in Master Leases, Building New Pre-Sold Buildings, Solve Property Financial Problems, Repair Properties, Sell Sub Divide Land and Sell Lots, Trust Deed Discounts, Joint Ventures, Make Loans, etc. Together with the many EGLPs each with a growing O&IF build-up over time, will allow all types of real estate investment.

PART 5
THE EQUITY RESCUE PROGRAM LEGAL SECTION

NOTICE: THE AUTHOR IS NOT A LAWYER!

Therefore, each interested person in the Equity Rescue Program should verify with an attorney the legal statements put forward herein. There are sources for anyone to check the meaning of any of the legal terms and the proper use of any legal items used in the EGLP. **Merriam-Webster's Dictionary of Law Definition is one, the internet is another, and there most likely is a law library close to you. Or call a lawyer! So, verify, verify, verify.**

EGLP LEGAL POSITION

In the Equity Rescue TDPP, there are established legal positions in the Articles of Partnership for the EGLP that are seldom used. These legal principles and laws used in the EGLP have never been designed or used together in combination in a partnership or investment before. This is a unique legal design that establishes a different and better method to rescue property equity for the owner. The design also creates a way for a qualified cash investor to invest through a limited partnership safely! NOTE: The laws and principles are all completely in law!

UNFAMILIAR MATERIAL

This original legal design/combination *is the key that opens the door* to several financial and investment revelations that are achieved in the Equity Rescue Program! The process in the TDPP uses the following legal statutes and regulations to create a unique legal operating structure. Special notice should be taken to the uniqueness of each legal usage working in combination for the very first time. This legal combination is original and not found in any other investment.

Here are terms used in the EGLP that are unusual to the real estate community. Some of these legal statutes and regulations are never used by real estate brokers in normal everyday sale activity. They are:

- A special Articles of Partnership (AP).
- A uniquely designed General Partner (GP) power of attorney in the AP.
- A special use for a Performance Trust Deed (PTD).
- A special use of the Bare Title principal of "non-possessory" ownership.
- A Grant Deed that holds title only to transfer to a new buyer as a fee title.
- A Condition Subsequent pledge of property in the AP.
- A use of Fee Simple Executory Limitation, a determinable fee.

THE "ONE AND ONLY" *LEGAL COMBINATION* THAT WILL WORK

The Equity Rescue "special legal design" makes it possible. Without the unique EGLP and its original set of Articles Of Partnership, a Power Of Attorney that includes a special fiduciary relationship created, a Bare Title/Equitable Title division of ownership rights, a Grant Deed with special required terms, use of Fee Simple Executory Limitation a Determinable Fee, a securing of a pledge with a Performance Trust Deed, and a Condition Subsequent agreement to transfer and sell property, it would not be possible to complete the "Trust Deed Pledge Plan" transaction. This is the only original legal scenario that will work to avoid foreclosure and rescued the total property equity, solely for the property owner's benefit. Without the unique comprehensive Legal arrangement, there would be no new type of investor providing money and no way to perform the transaction. It is the Legal structure that creates the PCI position, and the money needed to perform the transaction. No such Legal grouping for this purpose has ever been designed or achieved before!

Without this Legal structure, there would be no ability to raise large sums of <u>Operating and Investment Capital</u> on an ongoing repetitive basis to invest for profit.

LEGAL DIFFERENCE

In creating the EGLP/TDPP an original legal scenario had to be designed, one that has never been constructed for the same purpose and used in the same way. The plan achieves the purpose of rescuing real property equity from foreclosure for the owner's exclusive benefit. However, the main purpose of the plan is to collect large sums of investment capital into an Operating and Investment Fund for a Limited Partnership to invest and share profits with the owners / limited partners.

The TDPP has original language, investment structure, legal construction, and operational techniques that are new and different. These individual parts together in a unique plan of operation create an exceptional first-time ability and result. The unique techniques and advantages created have never been duplicated in any other real estate investment.

The EGLP/TDPP has a different legal configuration that affords both a currently financially insolvent property owner in foreclosure and a qualified cash investor a unique way to safely invest together. Rescuing property equity from being foreclosed and turning it into investment capital is what the TDPP does. The EGLP also raises large sums of capital to invest this way. The investment capital gathered is invested for the benefit of the owners rescued from foreclosure.

EGLP EXCLUSIVE LEGAL PERFORMANCE OUTLINE
THE "STEP BY STEP" LEGAL PROCESS

Steps of taking a property bare title and then transferring a fee simple ownership by grant deed to a new buyer. The following legal statutes are used to form a group that gives the EGLP the legal ability it needs to achieve its purpose.

Step 1 First Legal Item: The Articles of Partnership (AP) ©. The partners involved enter a legal contract, the Articles of Partnership. The cash investor, the property owner whose property is in foreclosure, and the General Partner of the EGLP all sign the AP. The AP sets out the purpose of each limited partner and is designed structurally in a unique way that creates an innovative legal position to achieve each limited partner's purpose. The AP creates a strong legal position so each limited partner can achieve its intended purpose. The AP dictates that the owner transfer the property's Bare Title to the EGLP to cure the foreclosure and hold the Bare Title until it is sold by the EGLP. The AP is drawn in such a way as to legally and financially allow this to happen. The AP describes and protects each partner's legal, financial, and investment position. The acknowledgment is accomplished at the escrow company's office.

The Articles of Partnership is the legal agreement between all the partners used to accomplish the purpose that they have all agreed on. It is a voluntary contract between and among a General Partner and persons who place their investment capital into an EGLP. The understanding is that there will be a sharing of the profits between the limited property owner investors and the EGLP. The PCI investor is to receive a pre-agreed fixed amount bonus for investing cash to cure the property, at a critical moment in time, to sell it for full value for the benefit of the owners.

A specially designed and newly constructed Limited Partnership is created in the EGLP which grants special advantages for just one class of limited partners, the PCI. There are two classes of limited partners in the EGLP, the property owner taken out of foreclosure being the other class. A unique legal, financial, and investment construction in a Limited Partnership, never achieved, is necessary to provide:

- A full value sale for the owner to rescue all the property equity from foreclosure for the sole benefit of the owner.
- A new secured cash investor position in the Partnership that makes investing in foreclosures safer and more rewarding than standard real estate investing.
- A new ever-growing never-ending investment capital fund is created by rescuing equities and investing them in the Partnership for the owners. This has been accomplished.

A fiduciary relationship is a relationship of trust that is established between the limited partners and the EGLP. The terms and conditions in the EGLP Articles of Partnership establish a fiduciary relationship (one of trust) between the partners and the EGLP general partner.

Step 2 Second Legal Item: Power of Attorney (AP). A power of attorney is a legal authority. The Power of Attorney granted to the General Partner in the Articles gives the power and responsibility to complete all the terms and conditions set down in the AP to the GP. The GP must adhere to the terms and conditions laid down in the AP. It directs the property in foreclosure to be taken out of foreclosure and sold by the EGLP. A contractual agreement is established by the AP that creates a fiduciary relationship for the GP with all the partners.

Step 3 Third Legal Item: Grant Deed. The EGLP first receives a Grant Deed transferring only the Bare Title to the property subject to terms and conditions in the AP. The property owner transfers the Bare Title to the EGLP to only hold the title for sale and disposition. The escrow records the transfer of the Grant Deed signed by the owner to the EGLP, as required in the escrow instructions and in the AP.

Explanation of deed: Blackstone defines a deed as a "writing or instrument under seal, containing some contract of agreement, and which the parties have delivered." Thus, the word "deed", in a legal sense, may mean any sealed contract or instrument, such as a lease, mortgage, or bond. The popular sense restricts it to a conveyance of property. A Grant Deed subject to terms and conditions that established what the grantor/grantee ownership is between them. A conveyance is a right, title, or interest in real or personal property from one person or entity to another. A deed may then be defined as writing by which lands, tenements, and hereditaments are conveyed, which writing is signed, sealed, and delivered by the parties. The ordinary common deed contains several clauses that have an important bearing on the rights of the parties.

Step 4 Fourth Legal Item: Bare Title.
EGLP Bare Title Understanding: A title can be passed from the Grantor to the Grantee without passing the full bundle of legal rights that must be understood. The bundle of legal rights consists of all the equitable ownership rights and the legal title to the property. No ownership equitable interest needs to pass if that is what is agreed to between the Grantor and Grantee. it is possible that the Grantor can transfer only the Bare Legal Title to the Grantee.

In property law, a title is a bundle of rights in a piece of property in which a person or entity may own either a legal interest or equitable interest. The rights in the bundle may be separated and held by different parties. Title may also refer to a formal document, such as a deed, that serves as evidence of ownership. Conveyance of the document may be required to transfer ownership in the property to another person. Title is distinct from possession, a right that often accompanies ownership but is not necessarily sufficient to prove it. In many cases, both possession and title may be transferred independently of each other. For real property, land registration and recording provide public notice of ownership information.

Ownership of property may be private, collective, or common, and the property may be of objects, land or real estate, or intellectual property. Determining ownership in law involves determining who has certain rights and duties over the property. These rights and duties, sometimes called a "bundle of rights", can be separated and held by different parties. The EGLP Articles of Partnership conditions the grant deed transfer from the owner to the EGLP with a Bare Title, a holding title position. The EGLP has no equitable ownership interest and by agreement is only holding the legal title for disposition.

Merriam-Webster Dictionary of Law Definition of TITLE: The means or right by which one owns or possesses property, broadly: the quality of ownership as determined by a body of facts and events. Bare title to the property lacks the usual rights and privileges of ownership. A trustee in a deed of trust securing instrument may hold the title to a secured property, but only such title as is needed to carry out the terms of the lien document.

In EGLP the property owner deposits the Grant Deed into escrow that transfers the Bare Title to the EGLP, as stipulated and agreed to in the AP by the owner. The EGLP AP conditions the grant deed transfer to the EGLP with a Bare Title "non-possessory" legal position. The EGLP with the Bare Title is to hold, sell and transfer the legal ownership on behalf of the owner to a new buyer and that is all.

The Bare title to the property lacks all the usual rights and privileges of ownership. The Owner/Grantor retains the equitable ownership in the "legal bundle of rights". The EGLP (the grantee) possesses "no ownership interest in the property" transferred. The EGLP Bare Title is a "holding only position" and it avoids taking or having any "ownership interest".

A trust exists whenever title to property is vested in one person to be held for the benefit of another. A trustee or fiduciary in a deed of trust securing instrument may hold the title to a secured property but only such title as is needed to carry to the terms of the lien document (contract). The EGLP will become the "legal title holder" when it receives the bare title from escrow. Bare title is a type of "non-possessory ownership". POSSESSION: The act or state of owning or holding "something".

The owner's purpose in transferring Bare Title to the EGLP is to have the "property fee ownership" pledged as collateral, after the is foreclosure is cured, to attract investment capital into the EGLP. Upon the Grant Deed Bare Title transfer to the EGLP the owner is fulfilling a condition laid down in the AP.

Equitable Title Is Title vested in one who is considered by the application of equitable principles to be the owner of property even though legal title is vested in another (the purchaser under a contract for sale had equitable title to and an insurable interest in the property; the right to receive legal title upon performance of an obligation).

You have the legal title if your name appears as the grantee on a deed. The legal title is "apparent" ownership or ownership that is documented on paper. You may assume that your ownership of a property is complete with legal title, but this is not the case. Another party may have equitable title restricting some of the ways you can use and enjoy the property.

The main difference between an equitable vs. a legal title is that the latter is the only one that gives actual ownership of the property. There are many smaller, more intricate differences that can vary on a case-by-case basis. In general, the equitable title gives a person the right to use the land and enjoy the benefits that come along with its ownership. The legal title does not necessarily grant these rights. An equitable title does not allow the titleholder to sell or transfer ownership. Legal title is the only title that can do this. In the TDPP the EGLP sells the property for the owner's benefit! Legal title has the advantage over equitable in that it allows the legal titleholder to demand compensation from parties that purchase or lease the property.

Equitable ownership is not "true ownership." In other words, someone with the equitable title could not argue that he or she was the legal owner or possessor of the property in a court of law. True ownership requires a legal title. The equitable title does, however, grant the person more consistent control over the property. That's right – equitable title can be more important than the legal title.

Step 5 Fifth Legal Item: Performance Trust Deed. A Performance Trust Deed or mortgage is security for the "performance of an act or obligation and therefore it may secure a money debt or any other obligation. Generally, it secures the obligations of a promissory note, but it also can secure other obligations of the trustor such as a lease, the performance of a contract, or future obligations created by contract or it can be used to indemnify the beneficiary against possible contingencies.

The EGLP gives into escrow a PTD in favor of the PCI and it is recorded against the property in the land recorder's office. A PTD secures a pledge of collateral (the property fee ownership) made to the PCI by the EGLP in the AP. The EGLP could not secure the collateral pledged, the property fee simple ownership, without first taking the Bare Title to transfer the ownership to a new buyer. There is a reference in the PTD identifying the necessary Articles in the AP that gives the legal right and responsibility to the GP to take the title and sell the property. The PTD secures the EGLP start-up funds provided by the PCI with the pledge of collateral to the PCI. The escrow records the transfer of the PTD as instructed to do in the escrow instructions.

Step 6 Sixth Legal Item: Fee Simple Executory Limitation: A defeasible fee created with clear durational language expressing a condition (e.g. "so long as", "until", "while"), which causes ownership of a property to vest in a third party identified by the grantor if that condition comes about. A Fee Simple Executory Limitation position is established in the AP to complete a Condition Subsequent created in the AP that mandates a sale of the property for the owners by the EGLP.

In the Trust Deed Pledge Transaction when the Condition Subsequent, specifically the sale of the property, the automatic right to transfer the property's fee simple title becomes possible. This right is established in the AP and the fee simple executory limitation position.

DEFINATIONS
Merriam-Webster Dictionary of Law Definition of Fee Simple: Simple without limitation (as to heirs) and unrestricted (as to transfer of ownership): a fee that is alienable (as by deed, will, or intestacy) and of potentially indefinite duration.
Merriam-Webster Dictionary of Law Definition of Executory Limitation: A limitation that creates an executory interest. (A fee simple subject to an executory limitation).
Defeasible Fee: An estate in land that may be divested from its current owner upon the occurrence of an event set forth by the grantor in the grantee. An estate in land that may be divested from its current owner upon the occurrence of an event set forth by the grantor in the grant. A Fee Simple Executory Limitation position is established in the EGLP Articles of Partnership to complete a Condition Subsequent created in the AP that mandates for the EGLP to take Bare Title and to sell the property for the owner's benefit.

A defeasible estate is created when a grantor transfers land conditionally. Upon the happening of the event or condition stated by the grantor. Because a defeasible estate always grants less than a full fee simple, a defeasible estate will always create one or more future interests.

A fee simple determinable is an estate that will end automatically when the stated event or condition occurs. A fee simple subject to an executory limitation is an estate that ends when a specific condition is met and then transfers to a third party. The interest will not revert to the grantor. If the condition is met, the grantee loses interest, and the third party gains it automatically.[2]

Merriam-Webster's Dictionary of Law Definition of Determinable Fee: A defeasible fee that terminates automatically upon the occurrence of a specified event. Three types of defeasible estates are the 1) fee simple determinable, 2) fee simple subject to an executory limitation or interest, and 3) fee simple subject to a condition subsequent.

Step 7 Seventh Legal Item: Condition subsequence refers to an event or situation that brings an end to something else. A condition subsequent is often used in a legal context as a marker bringing an end to one's legal rights or duties. A condition subsequent may be either an event or a situation that must either (1) occur or (2) fail to continue to occur. When the Condition Subsequent, specifically the sale of the property, is completed the automatic right to transfer the property's fee simple title is established in the EGLP Article of Partnership and law.

In the Articles of Partnership, there is set up a Condition Subsequence that instructs the EGLP General Partner to arrange for the sale of the property for the owner. And when the sale occurs to deliver the fee simple ownership of the property by Grant Deed to a new owner. When the Condition Subsequent, specifically the sale of the property by the Partnership, is completed the automatic right to transfer the property's fee simple title is established in law and Articles of Partnership.

Step 8 Eighth Legal Item:
Real Estate Sales Contract. The EGLP lists and sells, through a real estate broker, the owner's property and transfers by Grant Deed Fee Simple Ownership of the property to the new owner.

SEVERAL OTHER NEW LEGAL RIGHTS ARE INCLUDED FOR A PCI
This is a first-time ever legal grouping:
Two Separate legal standings for the PCI:
- Articles of Partnership.
- Performance Trust Deed.

Five legal rights granted to the PCI in the EGLP are:
- Limited Partner
- Collateral Right by Grant Deed
- Performance Trust Deed
- Priority Use Privilege
- Collateral System Avoids Foreclosure and Bankruptcy

EGLP/TDPP MAJOR ORIGINAL LEGAL PERFORMANCE
The following legal advantages cannot be accomplished in any other Limited Partnership, or real estate transaction of any kind, without the legal grouping, described herein. The EGLP creates and provides the following new advantages that were never possible:

- A safe and legal way of advancing funds to cure a foreclosure for the owner so the owner could pay the current loan arrearages when no lender would lend more money to the owner.
- Having a Limited Partnership act in an original legal way, representing two different classes of partners, to accomplish their purposes.
- Using a "Performance Deed of Trust" in an original way, to bring one cash investor limited partner together in an EGLP with other types of limited partners needing financial help. Both of their needs, intentions, and desires can be accomplished.
- Legally establishing a new type of collateral concept by creating a "Priority Loss Position" for one partner in a Limited Partnership.
- Legally establishing two ways to be successful for an investor in a Limited Partnership. The investor gets the reward or collection of substantial collateral, one or the other!
- Establishing a legal right to "property title fee ownership", not just an "equity lien position", to protect the investor capital invested.
- Creating a new reward system and paying one partner first with a pre-agreed amount of reward while other partners share Partnership profits.
- Changing a financially non-qualified insolvent investor (property owner in foreclosure) into a legally qualified cash investor in an EGLP.
- Arranging a new fast and easier legal method to collect the investor reward or property collateral by creating two legal standings in an EGLP.
- The EGLP has an original legal structure designed to achieve the purpose of rescuing equities from foreclosure and investing the equities for the property owner. (This one has never been done before and is a new legal structure inside a Limited Partnership)
- Creates two legal classes of limited partners with different contributions, and financial and legal positions in the Partnership. (This one has never been done before in this way and is a new legal structure inside a Limited Partnership)
- Combines two different legal standings in the same investment. The Articles of Partnership and the Performance Trust Deed each offers a different legal standing to protect the investor. (This one has never been done before and is a new legal structure inside a Limited Partnership)
- Creates a new legal method to secure a single limited partner cash investor inside a Limited Partnership while not securing the other limited partners. (This one has never been done before and is a new legal structure inside a Limited Partnership)
- Created a new legal reward system to pay two different classes of limited partners in different ways in the same partnership. (This one has never been done before and is a new legal structure inside a Limited Partnership)
- Created a new sequence of legal events that feature new uses for several legal definitions of law that when combined create a new way of curing a foreclosure and rescuing property equity from loss, for the sole benefit of the property owners. (This one has never been done before and is a new legal structure inside a Limited Partnership)
- Created a new legal way for a cash investor to invest in Trust Deeds without being concerned about being involved in a legal, costly, and time-consuming foreclosure or bankruptcy action to collect the collateral behind the Trust Deed. (This one has never been done before and is a new legal structure inside a Limited Partnership)

HIGHLIGHTING THE EXCLUSIVE LEGAL ADVANTAGES.

These legal advantages cannot be accomplished in any other Limited Partnership, without the legal grouping described herein. The EGLP creates and provides the following new and exciting advantages that were never possible:

- A safe and legal way of advancing funds to cure a foreclosure for the owner, when no lender would lend more money to the owner, so the owner could pay the current loan arrearages.
- Having a Limited Partnership act as a legal force in an original way representing both classes of partners to accomplish their personal needs and intentions.
- Using a Performance Deed of Trust in a new way, to be able to bring partners with different roles together in a Limited Partnership, and to be able to accomplish the needs, intentions, and desires of both type of partners.
- Legally establishing a new type of collateral concept by creating a "Priority Use Position" for one partner in a Limited Partnership.
- Legally establishing second ways to be successful for an investor in a Limited Partnership, insuring a very low investment risk factor. The investor gets the reward or the collateral one or the other!
- Establishing a legal right to property title fee ownership, not just an equity lien position, as collateral for the PCI invested capital in a Limited Partnership.
- Creating a new reward system and paying one partner first with a pre-agreed fixed amount of reward while other partners in the Limited Partnership must wait to share Partnership profits.
- Changing a financially non-qualified insolvent investor (property owner in foreclosure) into a legally qualified cash investor in a Limited Partnership.
- Arranging a new legal method of collection of the reward promised by creating two legal standings for a secured cash investor in a Limited Partnership.

SUMMATION OF THE EGLP/TDPP PERFORMANCE
Here are some abilities the EGLP has:
- General Partner takes only Bare Title to the property.
- Rescues equity from being lost because of a foreclosure in a new way.
- Creates a secured transaction in a limited partnership for one cash investor.
- Introduces "secured investor" funds that are used to cure the foreclosure and rescue the property equity.
- Arranges a different risk-reward scenario for partners in the partnership.
- Makes investing very safe and rewarding with new legal and investment techniques.
- Arranges millions of investment dollars to invest.
- Favors one Partner's legal and investment position.
- Arranges two separate contractual positions for the PCI.
- Arranges a pledge of a "foreclosure free" fee ownership of a property chosen by the investor as collateral.
- Grants an EGLP Performance Trust Deed (PTD) in favor of the PCI and records it against the collateral property chosen by the PCI.
- Changes a financially insolvent property owner into a "cash investor" by having the owner use the rescued equity as investment capital in the EGLP.
- Invests and grows the rescued equity for the owner's benefit.
- Cures the foreclosure on the property chosen by the PCI and the property is no longer in foreclosure.
- Changes the value of the property, it becomes market value as the property is no longer in foreclosure subject to low offers.
- Changes a sale under duress of foreclosure that would be a give-a-way for pennies on the dollar into a "marketplace full value sale" for the owner.

- Establishes an EGLP financial support plan to insures property loan payments will be made, if necessary.
- Supplies the collateral security in place before the PCI places money into the escrow!
- Generates and grows a partnership "Operating and Investment Fund" accomplished by rescuing property equities from foreclosure and turning the equities into the owner's investment capital in the EGLP.
- Arranges new money in the EGLP and uses the TDPP for solutions to various financially troubled properties and new investments.
- Originates first-time investment transactions and improves standard transactions with substantial capital available to make it possible.
- Creates a new way to use a Performance Trust Deed to secure a pledge of property ownership
- Has the ability to interact EGLPs as tenant-in-common.
- Has the ability to solve financially troubled property problems.
- Has the ability to handle high-value property in foreclosure.

I hope I have been able to show you that without the "legal combination" arranged and developed in the TDPP, the rescue of 100% of property equity from a foreclosure cannot happen. The new way to invest safely in a pending foreclosure property and the new way to grow the operating and investment capital fund also would not be possible!

PART 6
EGLP PROFIT OPPORTUITIES

Using the property owner investment funds (rescued equity turned into investment funds) the EGLP invests for profit that is shared with the property owner turned into a limited partner investor. EGLP earns by investing in Master Leases, Building New Pre-Sold Buildings, solving Property Financial Problems, Repairing Difficult Problem Properties, Selling Sub-Divided Lots, Buying Discounted Trust Deeds, Joint Ventures, Make Loans, etc. Together with the many EGLPs each with a growing O&IF build-up over time, will allow all types of real estate investment. Many commissions and fees will result from the EGLP investments.

REAL ESTATE BROKERS FIRST-TIME EVER EARNING ADVANTAGES
New achievements:
- Brokers can now create a "safe" listing of property taken out of the foreclosure to sell, where before in the foreclosure process it was once very risky to handle.
- Brokers for the first-time in new ways can earn new types of referral fees and real estate commissions.
- Brokers can now for the first-time help a client solve a serious foreclosure financial problem by coordinating with the Equity Rescue Program.
- Brokers can now be associated with a plan that will have in time many different types and priced properties listed for sale will raise partnership operating and investment capital.
- For the first-time the combination of many properties for sale and investment capital control at the same time will allow Brokers to complete various real estate transactions in ways never contemplated

FIRST-TIME WAYS TO EARN EGLP/TDPP FEES AND COMMISSIONS
- Privilege Cash Investor earns $25,500 to $42,500 in one year.
- 1% of the EGLP property sales price for overseeing property listing.
- 5% of an EGLP property proceeds for finding property.
- $4,500 or $9,000 for procuring a PCI.
- $15,000 for raising $60,000 in a group of investors.
- As an investor in, or organizer of, a Group Limited Partnership that raises PCI money, in small amounts, to invest as one PCI in an EGLP.
- As an EGLP representative exclusive listing and sales.
- As a better Joint Venture Partner arrangement with EGLP.
- As a head of various types of Equity Rescue Investment seminars.
- EGLP property sales & listings commissions.
- Procure EGLP investment property.

A REAL ESTATE COMMISSION FOR FINDING, LISTING AND SELLING
Your real estate company gets the listing because you found the foreclosure property for the EGLP. So, your company listing fee is 6%: so, figure your listing commission on a $300,000 sale. Listing and sale commission 6% of sale price (6% of 300,000 = $18,000).
- An EGLP property fees and commission can add up to 8%.
- $ 3,500 5% of Net Sales Proceeds is the Finder Fee.
- $ 3,000 1% Listing property to sell and overseeing the listing.

- $18,000 6% Broker listing and selling fee.
- $24,500 Total earnings.

$24,000 is the total fees and commission involved in procuring and selling one EGP property valued at $300,000 for an EGLP. $24,500 divided by $300,000 equals = eight (8%) for one EGLP property.

YOU TAKE CONTROL OF PCI INVESTMENT GROUP

If you act as the GP and raise at least $60,000 from small amounts invested by several investors you will earn a $15,000 procuring fee plus 25% of the group Partnership profits for procuring the PCI group. The group partnership earning is in the form of a 42.5% bonus paid by the EGLP. The $15,000 is a one-time fee paid by the EGLP.

"Become one of the investors yourself with the $15,000 fee and 25% profit earned or stay as a GP and repeat with the same group again! Automatic repetitive origination fee opportunities from the same, already formed, investment group can occur under contract to do several EGLPs with the same investor group.

EARNING A BONUS AS A PCI INVESTOR

Regular PCI Bonus Program Example
Minimum – Maximum Bonus Program Example
$60,000 minimum times 42.5% equals $25,500 PCI bonus.
$100,000 maximum times 42.5% equals $42,500 PCI bonus.

ACCELERATED BONUS PROGRAM EXAMPLE

Investing in a second EGLP as a PCI. $60,000 plus $25,500 bonus equal $85,500 invested. $85,500 times 42.5% equals $36,337 for second EGLP bonus.
$100,000 is the limit for starting an EGLP.

EARNINGS AS AN EQUITY GROWTH PARTNER

The owner turned into a limited partner receives a share of Equity Growth Limited Partnership net profit. All owners share 75% of the EGLP profit.

COMMISSIONS AND FEES SCHEDULE EXAMPLES
EARNING FOR FINDING A PCI

You present the ER opportunity to an investor. The Finder origination fee is $9,000. $3000 is paid out of each of the first three properties sold by the EGLP.

For referring a PCI to the EGLP general partner: GP presents the opportunity. If you bring an investor to the GP, and the GP presents a plan to the investor, the referring person will receive an origination referral fee of $4,500. ($9,000 fee is split 50-50).

FOR FINDING PROPERTY

If you find an EGP that comes into the Partnership, then you will receive a Finder fee equal to FIVE percent (5%) of net proceeds sale when the Partnership sells the property.
- **EXAMPLE:** Property net sale proceeds are $70,000. The finder Fee is 5% of the $70,000. So, the amount of the Finder Fee is $3,500

FOR COORDINATING AND OVERSEEING AN EGLP PROPERTY LISTING.
For coordinating with the listing broker on the property the EGLP must sell, you receive 1% of the property Sale Price.

- **EXAMPLE**: 1% of the $300,000 sales price is $3,000.

OTHER EXCLUSIVE COMMISSIONS, FEES, AND REFERRALS WITHIN THE EGLP
Other income avenues:

- Sale of EGP/Partnership property---Listing Commission
- Sale of EGP/Partnership property---Sales Commission
- Partnership Property purchase for Investment---Represent Buyer Commission
- Partnership Property sale of Investment---Represent Seller Commission
- Leasing Fee (Master leases are very lucrative)
- Management Fee

It is exciting to see so many ways to personally earn through the plan. A nationwide referral program can bring many people who will enjoy earning by helping other people is serious need.

OPPORTUNITY IS HERE
Investing as everyone knows is a great venture to be involved in. It takes a lot of careful investigating and a risk factor. As everyone wants to be an investor it is difficult for the average American. Sometimes though a good opportunity comes along and bingo a way is found to start investing.

APPENDIX

Additional Information & Infographics

How The EGLP Uses The CCC and How It Is Replenshied After Each Sale

EGP Capital

Step 1: Property Qualification To Start

1) Appraisal value of foreclosure property	- $	321,000
2) Minus loan arrearage	- $	9,600
3) Minus all loans	- $	215,070
4) Estimate of "Gross" Equity	**$**	**96,330**

$60,000
* -$9,600
$50,400

Step 2: Estimate of EGP's Net Equity and "Initial" Capital Account Balance After Entry Into The EGLP

5) Available Equity (from Line 4)	$	96,330
6) Minus 7% outside broker sales commission	- $	22,470
7) Minus sales preparation	- $	3,000
8) Minus transfer closing costs	- $	4,000
9) EGP's "Initial" Capital Account	**$**	**66,860**

$50,400
* -$3,000
* -$4,000
$43,400

Step 3: Actual Sale of EGLP Property To Public

10) Sales's Gross Equity (L2+L4)		$105,930
11) Minus this sale's closing costs	- $	4,000
12) Minus 7% commission	- $	22,470
13) Minus CCC replenishment amount (L2+L7+L8)	- $	16,600
14) "Final" Capital Account Balance for EGP	**$**	**62,860**

Step 4: Cash from sale used to replenish CCC fund

15) CCC reserve balance at the time of sale	$43,400
16) * Proceeds from the sale replenish the CCC monies used above (L13)	+$16,600
17) CCC is totally replenished after each EGLP sale	**$60,000**

The Debt to Asset Ratio or "DAR" Formula

The DAR formula accounts for an EG Partnership's debt to asset ratio. The lower the percentage of debts to assets the safer the EG Partnership investment becomes for it Limited Partners. It is one of the methods we use to measure the safety factor of the EG Partnership.

EG Partnership First Property DAR Calculation

1st property value and debt

$	300,000	Appraised property value
-$	210,000	Total of current loans
=$	90,000	Gross equity in property

EG Partnership's Assets of Cash and Property Value

$	300,000	Property Value
+$	60,000	EG Partnership cash (CCC)
=$	360,000	EG Partnership total assets (Property & Cash)

$	210,000	EG Partnership total debts (1st property total current loans)
÷$	360,000	EG Partnership total assets
=	58.%	**DAR**

$360,000 Assets
58% DAR

The first property is sold. The $90,000 gross equity generates a $60,000 net equity which is added to the EG Partnership's asset base. Arriving at the $60,000 includes the full replenishment of the CCC fund. The $60,000 is figured into the acquisition of the second EG Partnership property and its DAR formula calculation.

EG Partnership Second Property DAR Calculation

2nd property value and debt

$	300,000	Appraised property value
-$	210,000	Total of current loans
=$	90,000	Gross equity in property

EG Partnership's Assets of Cash and Property Value

$	300,000	Property Value
+$	60,000	EG Partnership cash (CCC)
+$	60,000	EG Partnership asset (Cash: 1st property net equity)
=$	420,000	EG Partnership total assets (Property & Cash)

$	210,000	EG Partnership total debts (2nd property total current loans)
÷$	420,000	EG Partnership total assets
=	50.%	**DAR**

$420,000 Assets
50% DAR

The second property is sold. The $90,000 gross equity generates a $60,000 net equity which is added to the EG Partnership's asset base. Arriving at the $60,000 includes the full replenishment of the CCC fund. The $60,000 is figured into the acquisition of the third EG Partnership property and its DAR formula calculation.

EG Partnership Third Property DAR Calculation

3rd property value and debt

$	300,000	Appraised property value
-$	210,000	Total of current loans
=$	90,000	Gross equity in property

EG Partnership's Assets of Cash and Property Value

$	300,000	Property Value
+$	60,000	EG Partnership cash (CCC)
+$	60,000	EG Partnership asset (Cash: 1st property net equity)
+$	60,000	EG Partnership asset (Cash: 2nd property net equity)
=$	480,000	EG Partnership total assets (Property & Cash)

$	210,000	EG Partnership total debts (3rd property total current loans)
+$	480,000	EG Partnership total assets
=	44.%	DAR

The third property is sold. The $90,000 gross equity generates a $60,000 net equity which is added to the EG Partnership's asset base. Arriving at the $60,000 includes the full replenishment of the CCC fund.

At this point $180,000 in net equities is raised. The $25,500 Bonus is paid to the PCI, this leaves $154,500 in EG Partnership cash. The PCI also receives back the CCC. Both are figured into the acquisition of the fourth EG Partnership property and its DAR formula calculation.

EG Partnership Fourth Property DAR Calculation

4th property value and debt

$	300,000	Appraised property value
-$	210,000	Total of current loans
=$	90,000	Gross equity in property

EG Partnership's Assets of Cash and Property Value

$	300,000	Property Value
+$	154,500	EG Partnership asset (Cash remaining after bonus is paid)
=$	454,500	EG Partnership total assets (Property & Cash)

$	210,000	EG Partnership total debts (4th property total current loans)
+$	454,500	EG Partnership total assets
=	46.%	DAR

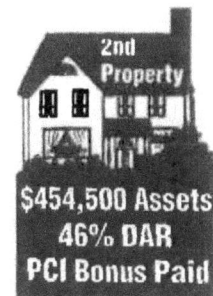

This formula continues in this cycle of dividing debts by accumulating assets. What is important to realize is that the DAR Formula assesses the safety factor for both the PCI and the EGPs. While the PCI only stays in the EG Partnership after to the third or fourth sale of EG Partnership property the EGP will experience much lower DAR Formula percentages. The EG Partnership will continue to make "nonpurchase" acquisitions of EGP contributed properties and build its asset base. The lower the Debt to Asset Ratio percentage the safer the investment.

Raising Investment Capital For One EGLP

The process can continue to until the EGLP has enough partners.

Beyond that the assets of the partnerhip can be contained combined with other EGLPs.

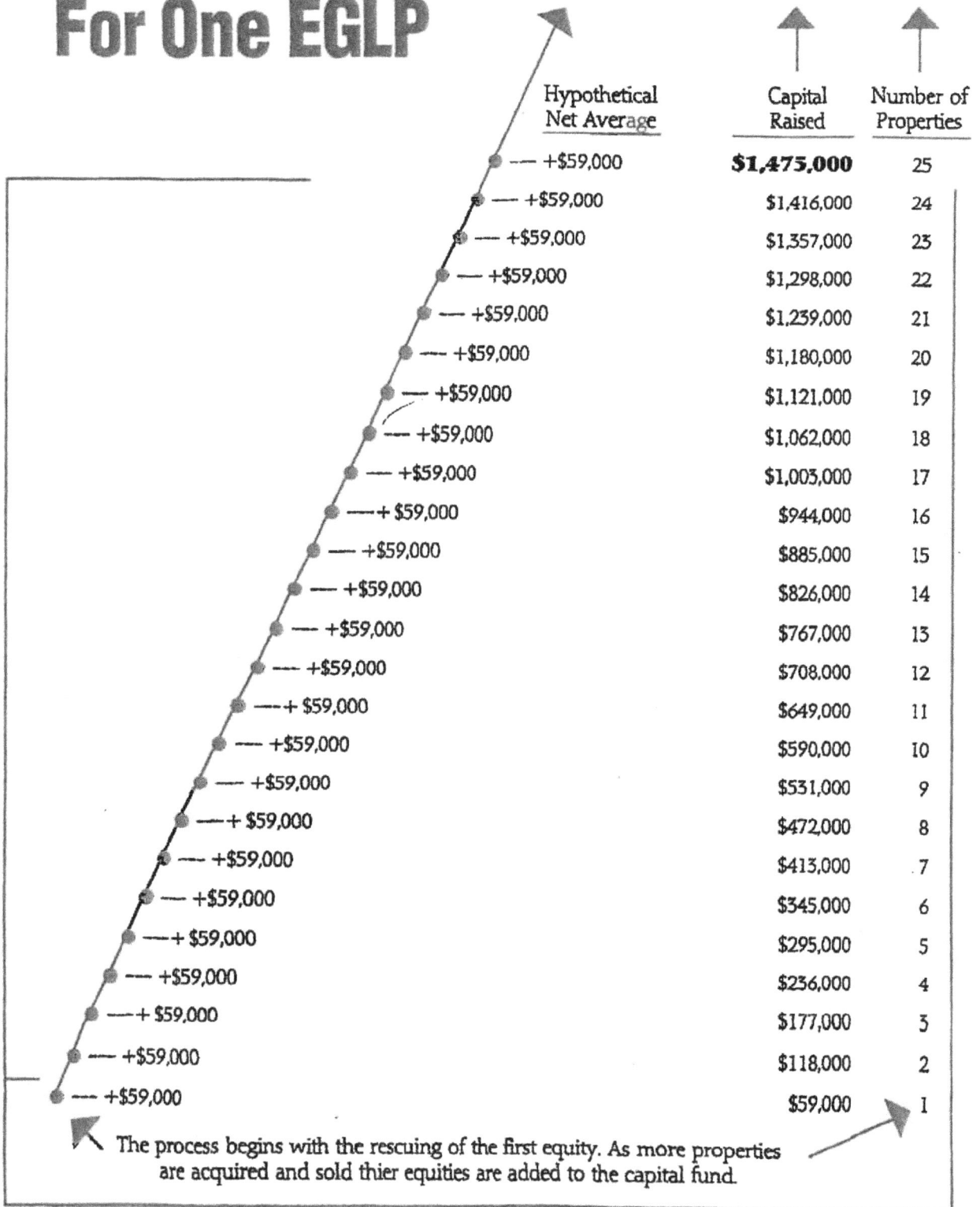

Hypothetical Net Average	Capital Raised	Number of Properties
+$59,000	**$1,475,000**	25
+$59,000	$1,416,000	24
+$59,000	$1,357,000	23
+$59,000	$1,298,000	22
+$59,000	$1,239,000	21
+$59,000	$1,180,000	20
+$59,000	$1,121,000	19
+$59,000	$1,062,000	18
+$59,000	$1,003,000	17
+$59,000	$944,000	16
+$59,000	$885,000	15
+$59,000	$826,000	14
+$59,000	$767,000	13
+$59,000	$708,000	12
+$59,000	$649,000	11
+$59,000	$590,000	10
+$59,000	$531,000	9
+$59,000	$472,000	8
+$59,000	$413,000	7
+$59,000	$345,000	6
+$59,000	$295,000	5
+$59,000	$236,000	4
+$59,000	$177,000	3
+$59,000	$118,000	2
+$59,000	$59,000	1

The process begins with the rescuing of the first equity. As more properties are acquired and sold thier equities are added to the capital fund.

25 California EGLP's will Raise $36,875,000 in Investment Capital by Rescuing Equities

The process can continue throughout the United States and will in time save thousands and thousands of equities in many EGLP's.

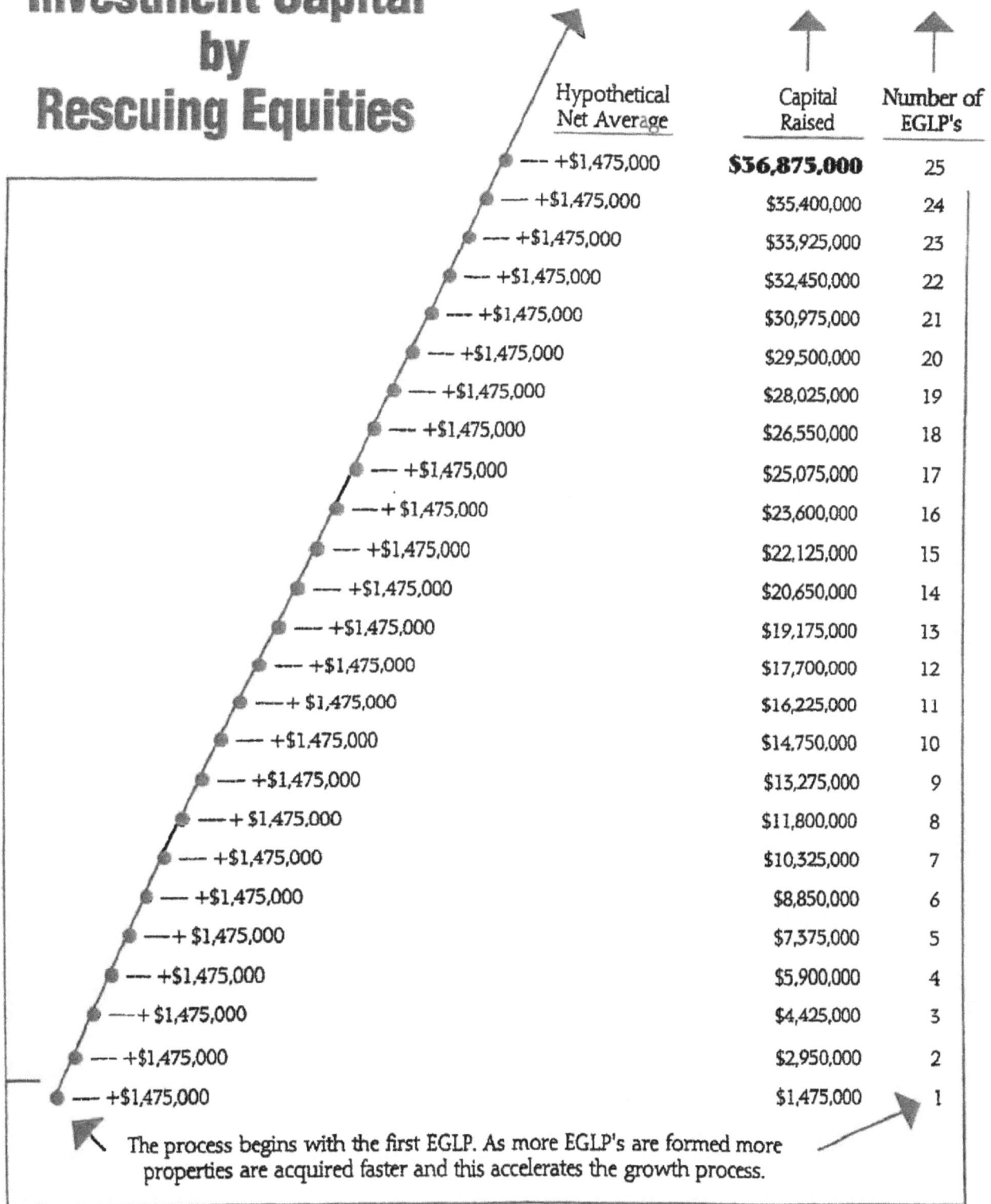

Hypothetical Net Average	Capital Raised	Number of EGLP's
+$1,475,000	**$36,875,000**	25
+$1,475,000	$35,400,000	24
+$1,475,000	$33,925,000	23
+$1,475,000	$32,450,000	22
+$1,475,000	$30,975,000	21
+$1,475,000	$29,500,000	20
+$1,475,000	$28,025,000	19
+$1,475,000	$26,550,000	18
+$1,475,000	$25,075,000	17
+$1,475,000	$23,600,000	16
+$1,475,000	$22,125,000	15
+$1,475,000	$20,650,000	14
+$1,475,000	$19,175,000	13
+$1,475,000	$17,700,000	12
+$1,475,000	$16,225,000	11
+$1,475,000	$14,750,000	10
+$1,475,000	$13,275,000	9
+$1,475,000	$11,800,000	8
+$1,475,000	$10,325,000	7
+$1,475,000	$8,850,000	6
+$1,475,000	$7,375,000	5
+$1,475,000	$5,900,000	4
+$1,475,000	$4,425,000	3
+$1,475,000	$2,950,000	2
+$1,475,000	$1,475,000	1

The process begins with the first EGLP. As more EGLP's are formed more properties are acquired faster and this accelerates the growth process.

Equity
Rescue

FINANCIAL STRUCTURAL CHARTS©

THE PERFORMANCE TRUST DEED©

Property 1 - PCI Receives Performance Trust Deed
In the first property sale escrow, the PCI re-conveys the PTD to the EGLP.

Property 2 - PCI Receives Performance Trust Deed
In **MORE THAN ONE PROPERTY AT A TIME HAS A PTD** the second property sale escrow, the PCI re-conveys the PTD to the EGLP.

Property 3 - PCI Can Get Several Property Performance Trust Deeds Until Three Properties Are Sold
After the first sale is made the EGLP can take in two properties at a time. The PCI will receive a PTD on both properties. After the second sale the EGLP will even be able to take in more properties looking to sell the third property. For each property taken into the EGLP the PCI will receive a PTD until three properties sell. So, when the third property is sold, the PCI will have to re-convey all PTD'S held.

THE EQUITY GROWTH LIMITED PARTNERSHIP©
PCI COLLATERAL ACCELERATES AND LOWERS RISK

Property 1 - $60,000 PCI Funds invested in the EGLP
Property Gross Equity of $100,000 in property 1
Total = Cash & Equity of $160,000 secures PCI $60,000

Property 2 - $60,000 is replenished from Property 1 sale
+ Property Gross Equity of $100,000 in Property 2
+ $70,000 Sale funds netted from Property 1 sale
Total = Cash and Equity of $230,000 secures PCI $60,000

Property 3 - $60,000 replenished from Property 2 sale
+ Property Gross Equity of $100,000 in Property 3
+ $70,000 Sale funds netted from Property 1
+ $65,000 Sale funds netted from Property 2
Total = Cash and Equity of $295,000 secures PCI $60,000

As you can see from this chart each time an EGLP sells a property the risk factor goes down for the PCI. Every investment has risked no matter how small the risk! However, this formula creates an extremely low risk for the PCI that would be hard to duplicate in other investments.

THE PRIVILEGE CASH INVESTOR©
THE PCI $60,000 INVESTED IS REPLENISHED AFTER EACH PROPERTY SALE

STEP 1: PROPERTY FINANCIAL STATUS
L1) $321,000 APPRAISAL VALUE & SALE PRICE BOTH
L2) $ 9,600 Minus Loan Arrearage (CCC USED)
L3) $215,070 Minus All Loan Amounts
L4) $ 96,330 ESTIMATE OF "GROSS" EQUITY

STEP 2: ESTIMATE OF QWNER'S "NET EQUITY"
L5) $ 96,330 AVAILABLE GROSS EQUITY **(L4)**
L6) $ 22,470 minus 7% broker commission
L7) $ 3,000 minus sales preparation (CCC USED)
L8) $ 4,000 minus title transfer cost to EGLP (CCC USED)
L9) $ 66,860 BALANCE IS NET EQUITY AFTER SALE

STEP 3: ACTUAL SALE OF THE PROPERTY TO A NEW BUYER
L10) $105,930 SALE GROSS EQUITY **(L2 plus L4)**
L11) $ 4,000 minus sales closing costs (directly from sale proceeds)
L12) $ 22470 minus 7% commission
L13) $ 16,600 minus CCC replenishment **(L2 plus L7 plus L8)**
L14) $ 62,860 NET EQUITY AFTER SALE

STEP 4: MONEY USED FROM THE CCC FUND IS REPLENISHED
$60,000 CCC fund
$ 9,600 minus loan arrears **(L2)**
$ 3,000 minus sales preparation **(L7)**
$ 4,000 minus title transfer cost to the EGLP **(L8)**
$43,400 The balance after expenses paid out of the CCC fund
$16,600 CCC fund is replenished out of the property sale proceeds
$60,000 ORIGINAL CCC FUND STARTING AMOUNT

EGLP CAPITAL ACCOUNT FOR EGP AFTER SALE
$105,930 Gross equity to start
$ 43,070 Total selling expense **(L11 + L12 + L13)**
$ 62,860 Net equity equals capital account balance

THE EQUITY GROWTH LIMITED PARTNERSHIP©
PCI BONUS ACCELERATION CHART

	Amount Invested	Bonus	Total Bonus Earned	Timing to Complete Each EGLP
1st EGLP Completed	$60,000	$25,500	$25,500	Approximately Three Months
2nd EGLP Completed	$85,500	$36,337	$61,837	Approximately Nine Months
3rd EGLP Completed	$121,337	$51,568	$113,405	*Approximately One Year*

THE EQUITY GROWTH LIMITED PARTNERSHIP©
PCI BONUS ACCELERATION CHART

	Amount Invested	Bonus	Total Bonus Earned	Timing to Complete Each EGLP
1st EGLP Completed	$100,000	$42,500	$42,500	Approximately Three Months
2nd EGLP Completed	$100,000	$42,500	$85,000	Approximately Nine Months
3rd EGLP Completed	$100,000	$42,500	$127,500	*Approximately One Year*

Requires 5 EGLP sales to be completed.

Robert L. Evans
Real Estate Broker
r.leeevans@aol.com

www.ingramcontent.com/pod-product-compliance
Lightning Source LLC
Chambersburg PA
CBHW052344210326
41597CB00037B/6251